FRAUD

FRAUD

How the Left Plans to Steal the Next Election

Eric Eggers

of the
Government Accountability Institute

REGNERY PUBLISHING
A Division of Salem Media Group

Regnery® is a registered trademark of Salem Communications Holding Corporation

Cataloging-in-Publication data on file with the Library of Congress

ISBN 978-1-62157-795-9
e-book ISBN 978-1-62157-838-3

Published in the United States by
Regnery Publishing
A Division of Salem Media Group
300 New Jersey Ave NW
Washington, DC 20001
www.Regnery.com

Manufactured in the United States of America

10 9 8 7 6 5 4 3 2 1

Books are available in quantity for promotional or premium use. For information on discounts and terms, please visit our website: www.Regnery.com.

To Fran Thompson

CONTENTS

Foreword

By Peter Schweizer

lthough we love to complain about the campaign ads, the long lines at the polls, and all the signs that litter the roadways like falling leaves, we Americans vote. We do it to teach our children how to be good citizens, to keep "them" from getting into office, and to feel a stronger connection with our town, state, and nation. We trudge to the polls in November and tap screens, flip levers, and fill in circles on paper ballots with our #2 pencils.

Voting is a duty, and a right, that men and women have died for. It is an accomplishment and a reminder that we are *consenting* to be governed by choosing our own leaders. Voting is a civil right and a solemn obligation not to take government of, by, and for the people for granted.

It also expresses our trust that our vote will count as much as anyone else's, and that it will be cast fairly, tabulated accurately,

1

and honored by everyone. As Americans, we're born or become citizens knowing all of that, and we guard it jealously. I once saw a t-shirt that read simply: "MY VOTE CANCELS OUT Y'ALLS."

So, when the subject of voter fraud arises, our jealousy should be aroused. Americans, like free people everywhere, believe in fair play and respect for the rules. We should get fired up when there are credible allegations of vote fraud or ballot tampering. But the truth is that voting in America has long been tainted by documented cases of fraud and other "irregularities." We all have nagging suspicions that some votes were not cast legally, or that scheming political operatives have figured out how to exploit the process and rig an election.

You will read about some of the historical examples of that here. Eric Eggers's book will take you into the world of party bosses who treat the ballot box like a cookie jar, prey on elderly Americans and recent immigrants, and conspire to make sure elections go their way. They succeeded for years, even for decades in some cases.

There is an uncomfortable side to talking about voter fraud. But not to joking about it. "Vote early, vote often" is an old one. So are all the cracks about dead people in Chicago being the real "swing voters" in any Windy City election. For decades, New Jersey Governor Brendan Byrne joked that he wanted to be buried in Hudson County "so that I can remain active in Democratic politics." Perhaps the jokes are a way of acknowledging what most of us already suspect is true: voter fraud really does happen today.

Recent news stories have alleged that Russian intelligence agents tried to hack voter information systems in several states. Sensational charges that spies from other countries may have tried to crack into electronic voting systems themselves have been cited by several states as one reason they are returning to paper ballots and scanners. These attempts are a reminder that our voting systems must be absolutely secure from foreign interference. But what about interference by domestic bad actors?

This book exposes voter fraud that is all homegrown and has become routine in many parts of America. As you read Eric's findings, you will appreciate that there are many careers that owe their success to exploiting the vulnerabilities in the ways we vote. The techniques of fraud documented here are not hard to do, but they are hard to detect or investigate. That's by design. It's also why they are seldom prosecuted.

The problem is that these kinds of investigations take real effort, cooperation, objectivity, and determination. As you will see in this book, voter fraud can—and does—happen in many different ways. Whether it is done by stealing absentee ballots, inducing noncitizens to cast ballots illegally, voting in multiple states during the same election, or through other devious means, tracking down the perpetrators and proving the fraud is labor-intensive. As we discover at every turn, government agencies that are supposed to ensure the openness and integrity of our elections will throw up roadblocks to outsiders trying to look into these questions. Sometimes, politicians simply deny that a voter fraud problem even exists, or they minimize it, or they question the motives of those who seek the details. But few in government seem very eager to answer these basic questions: Is voter fraud widespread? What can we do to stop it?

Our organization, the Government Accountability Institute (GAI), was born in 2012 to do this kind of work, and ask these sorts of questions. We are a nonprofit group of investigative reporters, researchers, and writers who do our own research and publish our findings in reports, or as raw material shared with media organizations to pursue further, and as books like this one.

While many of the books we've written on government corruption and incompetence bear my name as the author, they all relied on our marvelous team at GAI. They are dogged, curious, skilled investigators who pose the questions, research the facts, and scrutinize the excuses of politicians of both parties. With the support of our generous donors, we do the legwork that reporters and editors at the major networks and largest newspapers *used* to do, but no longer have the resources or the time to do themselves.

Previous GAI investigations have exposed corruption in Congress, in the vast federal bureaucracy, in political candidates who enrich themselves and their family members through sweetheart deals and subtler forms of bribery. Our most recent book, *Secret Empires*, became a number one bestseller on the *New York Times* list. It reveals the many ways that members of Congress and even a president have enriched their children and closest friends, legally, by taking advantage of loopholes in financial disclosure laws that govern how *they* can earn money, but don't place any restrictions on their family members.

Time will tell if that book leads to changes, but its predecessor certainly did. *Clinton Cash: The Untold Story of How and Why Foreign Governments and Businesses Helped Make Bill and Hillary Rich* dogged Hillary Clinton's 2016 campaign for president with its investigation of the ways Bill and Hillary Clinton leveraged their nonprofit foundation empire for personal gain and engaged in numerous quid pro quo schemes to enrich their friends and donors. That book too was a *New York Times* bestseller, and it was quoted and cited extensively during the presidential campaign. It also was credited with spurring several FBI investigations into the Clinton Foundation and any favors Secretary Clinton may have done on behalf of Foundation donors. GAI's team spent nearly two years researching the stories told in that book, and we're proud of its success.

Earlier efforts took on Congress in *Throw Them All Out*, which documented how congressmen traded their own stock portfolios based on confidential information they learned in supposedly closed hearings. This led to passage of the STOCK Act, outlawing the practice. Our book *Extortion* showed how the Obama Administration targeted industries for criminal investigation but chose not to pursue key political donors, slid open the door to then-Speaker John Boehner's "Tollbooth," and how lawmakers used campaign slush funds to bankroll their lavish lifestyles complete with limos, private jets, golf at five-star resorts, fine wines, and cash for family members.

These GAI efforts all helped explain why our government is so dysfunctional: it's all about making money, not making law. *This* book, though, takes on political corruption of a different, related form. Where we have previously focused on how politicians enrich themselves once they get into office, Eric Eggers, Research Director at GAI, tackles the shady ways some of them get there. And stay there.

He will show you how some political operatives do all they can to open voting up to noncitizens living in their jurisdictions, and how they and their wealthy allies fight to block laws requiring voter ID. You will read stories of how *boleteros* and *politiqueros* broker the votes of senior citizens living in nursing homes in Florida and Texas. You'll come to understand that the fights over so-called Motor Voter bills and the current debate in Washington about whether the U.S. Census should ask if someone is a citizen are all about protecting the many strategies for perpetuating routine, reliable, tried-and-true methods of voter fraud.

There are hopeful signs that voter fraud in its many forms is being taken more seriously than in the past. In its first year in office, the Trump administration made one abortive attempt to study voter registration records from all fifty states. A bipartisan commission it created was rebuffed by opposition from many states, who still control this information and aren't eager to share it outside their borders, as we also found when we conducted our own analysis of the voting rolls of twenty-one states. Still, the connection of this issue to the immigration debate, and to the 2020 Census, will keep the questions and the demand for real answers coming. Eric's work, his first as an author, will make it harder to make excuses for avoiding honestly measuring the real extent of fraud in American elections. But, as any recovering alcoholic will tell you, the first step is admitting that you have a problem.

Eric's book is a great way to start.

Introduction

When I told a high-ranking Florida Cabinet-level official that I had uncovered 2,200 examples of double-voting in Florida during the 2016 elections, he replied: "I didn't realize there were that many lightning strikes that year." Like most academics and politicos on the Left, he dismissed voter fraud as a non-issue. When I told a friend with experience on many Democratic political campaigns that I was writing a book on voter fraud, he said, "I guess it's gonna be a short book."

Those who dismiss concerns about voter fraud often quote the Brennan Center for Justice at the New York University School of Law, a leading left-wing legal think tank. It concluded that "examination after examination of voter fraud claims reveal fraud is very rare, voter impersonation is nearly non-existent, and much of the problems associated with alleged fraud relates to unintentional mistakes by voters or election administrators."[1]

Actually, what "examination after examination of voter fraud claims reveal" is that *prosecutions* of voter fraud are very rare, in part because official local, state, or federal monitoring of voter rolls or election sites to find voter fraud are essentially nonexistent. And when people do point to apparent voter fraud, one of two things usually happens: they get ignored or they get called a racist. Both happened in one Florida County, when a supervisor of elections flagged two thousand absentee ballots or request forms as possibly fraudulent, and detectives with a state attorney's office found "clear cut evidence of voter fraud" yet the only charges filed were accusations of racial bias.[2]

Federal laws passed twenty-five years ago have left gaping vulnerabilities in America's highly localized system of voter registration, and I have found countless examples, from all regions of the country, of ineligible voters casting ballots. And these instances of illegal voting are not random, they are directed by political activists. As this book documents, there are highly organized and well-funded political organizations that share both a funding source and an overarching motivation to manipulate the electoral system for their benefit.

The same groups who fight against simple security measures like mandatory IDs at the polls or voter roll database verifications are winning political battles to remove the few safeguards to our voter registration system that do remain. In several cities across the country, including Chicago and San Francisco, it is now legal for noncitizens to vote in certain local elections.

When Donald Trump announced the formation of his Presidential Commission on Voter Reforms, and warned that millions of illegal votes could have been cast in the 2016 elections, the Brennan Center, and others, scoffed at the notion.

The Brennan Center is perhaps the leading high-profile denier of what it calls "the myth of voter fraud." But as this book will show, the Brennan Center has millions of reasons to dismiss and deny the mountains of evidence that voter fraud is all too real.

The Brennan Center—and for the most part, the media—define voter fraud in the narrowest of terms, saying voter fraud only "occurs when individuals cast ballots despite knowing that they are ineligible to vote, in an attempt to defraud the election system."[3]

As the *New York Times* notes, "Election law experts say that pulling off in-person voter fraud on a scale large enough to swing an election, with scores if not hundreds of people committing a felony in public by pretending to be someone else, is hard to imagine, to say nothing of exceptionally risky."[4]

But this is an ingenious and misleadingly narrow definition of voter fraud, which in reality goes far beyond individual ineligible voters. The *New York Times* acknowledged that "There are much simpler and more effective alternatives to commit fraud on such a scale," citing Yale law professor Heather Gerken, who observed, "You could steal some absentee ballots or stuff a ballot box or bribe an election administrator or fiddle with an electronic voting machine." That explains, she said, "why all the evidence of stolen elections involves absentee ballots and the like."

What this book will do is document the "and the like"—the many means and methods by which legal voters have their votes diluted or disenfranchised because of fraud. And it will examine the myriad ways the voting system fails to safeguard elections.

In 2017, after Donald Trump was inaugurated, he claimed millions of illegal votes had been cast against him, which contributed, in his estimation, to his loss in the popular vote to Hillary Clinton.

Trump's claim of fraudulent votes was immediately dismissed by establishment media and legal scholars who cited the statistics that purported to show that voter fraud, as defined by the Brennan Center and elsewhere, was "a myth." But a 2016 audit by state officials in North Carolina may have inadvertently provided evidence that people who shouldn't be voting are actually casting ballots in significant numbers, just not for reasons leftists want to count as "voter fraud."

A Huffington Post article on the findings claimed the audit revealed that just .01 percent of all votes cast were fraudulent. But even in its effort to minimize the threat of illegal voting, the article highlighted a larger point, finding that "In the 41 cases of noncitizens voting, for example, the Board of Elections found that all of the individuals were in the United States legally and didn't know they were prohibited from voting. Some had been misinformed by canvassers. One woman who had registered to vote had lived in the United States for 50 years and thought she had citizenship because she had been married to a U.S. citizen."[5]

This is exactly the point. By defining voter fraud as an *intentional* effort to impersonate another voter, voter fraud reductionists would not count the thousands of examples of noncitizens who illegally vote as voter fraud, because they didn't do so with an intention to impersonate another voter. But what this book will show is that in many instances, noncitizens are the unwitting victims of the deliberate neglect by election officials at the federal, state, and local levels.

The reality is, our elections are only as secure as our voter rolls. While the Left argues that the Trump campaign colluded with Russia to hack the 2016 election and the Right believes millions of noncitizens illegally participated in the last election, both would seem to agree that our voter rolls are anything but secure. Thanks in part to billionaire George Soros and his network, there has been a concerted effort to put anyone and everyone on a voter roll. Numerous states automatically register driver's license applicants to vote. Other states have DMV employees help applicants with limited English to fill out voter register forms. In New Jersey, to cite just one example, Cezarramo Guisande was registered to vote by a DMV employee—over the objections of Guisande's mother who was with him and said he was ineligible as a noncitizen. The

DMV employee said anyone with a green card was eligible—which was not true.[6]

Lawyer and journalist J. Christian Adams's Public Interest Legal Foundation has uncovered thousands of examples of noncitizens being registered to vote all over the country. And there are numerous political organizing groups, such as ACORN, Unidos (formerly known as La Raza), and CASA de Maryland, who get registered voters to the polls regardless of citizenship status. These groups, and others, also fight against any introduction of Voter ID laws, all while taking money from George Soros, who has interests of his own.

But it isn't just political nonprofits who use Soros money to push this agenda. Tom Perez, the head of the Democratic National Committee who used to run CASA de Maryland, has made expanding noncitizen voting rights a priority for the Democrats in upcoming elections, while simultaneously fighting against additional voter security measures. Perez's reign is just beginning. And Soros's support isn't going away anytime soon. The eighty-seven-year-old Soros recently transferred $18 billion of his personal wealth to his Open Society Foundations organization, ensuring his wealth will continue to support this cause well after his death.[7]

This book will expose just how vast Soros's effort is to control every aspect of this country's elections, and how his funding of groups like the Brennan Center—whose president is a former Clinton White House senior aide—is part of that effort. The Soros network, in tandem with like-minded media outlets, push a narrative that consistently downplays the threat of voter fraud and insists that even minimal efforts to strengthen the integrity of our elections are racist. This, in fact, has become a core Democratic Party talking point.

Democratic Congressman Steve Cohen of Tennessee, for example, complained that "In the name of protecting Americans from supposed in-person voter fraud, a fraud that is virtually non-existent,

States have been enacting voter ID laws. The real reason for these laws, however, has been anything but election integrity. It has been about partisan politics and discrimination."[8]

Democratic Senator Cory Booker of New Jersey claimed the Trump-proposed Presidential Commission on Voter Integrity "will be used and is designed to support policies that will suppress the vote in minority and poor communities across the United States."[9]

That, of course, is blatantly untrue—as could be seen in the 2017 U.S. Senate election in Alabama. Alabama has voter ID laws—and it also saw record levels of minority voters in that election, turning the Democratic talking point on its head.

Statistically, voter fraud may not mean "millions" of illegal votes as President Trump has claimed (though you'll read about several academic studies that suggest he may be right). But remember that the 2000 presidential election was decided by only 537 votes in Florida.

In 2018, Democrats claimed a massive victory in a high-profile congressional race when Conor Lamb was declared the winner with a 500-vote margin over Republican Rick Saccone in Western Pennsylvania, a vote that occurred only months after Pennsylvania Secretary of State Pedro Cortés resigned after it was discovered that thousands of ineligible voters—foreign nationals—were listed on statewide rolls. The problem was likely much larger than that: in Pennsylvania, as in the rest of the country, illegal voters are often discovered only after they self-report through their naturalization process.

So why didn't Saccone ask for a recount? Because Pennsylvania law requires the nearly impossible standard of three voters within the same local precinct to attest that they personally witnessed an electoral error or fraud being committed in order to have a recount.[10] Many states have similar quirks in their election laws. States and localities can set up their election laws as they see fit, but, to say the obvious, voter fraud should not be part of our electoral system at any level. The danger is, as we'll see, there are powerful groups that are trying to make it so.

The Future Is Now—Tom Perez

For Democrats, the 2016 election was an unmitigated disaster. The DNC, under former chair Debbie Wasserman Schultz, was at the forefront of the Democratic Party's spectacular loss to Donald J. Trump. Longtime Democratic strategist and DNC board member, Donna Brazile, later explained that Barack Obama's 2012 reelection effort bankrupted the DNC, allowing Hillary Clinton's 2016 campaign, flush with cash, to take over the DNC and tilt the Democratic Party's nominating system away from her primary opponent, Vermont Senator Bernie Sanders.[1]

In the general election, a surprising number of traditional, blue-collar Democrats in Ohio, Michigan, Wisconsin, and Pennsylvania voted for Trump. They did so because of his positions on immigration and trade, and because the Democratic Party's extreme social liberalism and racial "identity politics" alienated them. Instead of trying to woo these Reagan Democrat voters back with targeted policies, incoming DNC chairman Tom Perez has accelerated the Party's left-wing trajectory.

Tom Perez represents the chosen future of the Democratic Party. The son of Dominican immigrants, Perez became the first ever Latino DNC chair after fending off a close challenge from Minnesota Congressman Keith Ellison, who would have been the DNC's first Muslim-American chairman. Both men come from the far Left of the party, although Perez remained a Clinton loyalist during the campaign, and had the backing of fellow Harvard Law School alum, Barack Obama. Ellison become deputy chairman.

Perez aims to lead a more aggressive, more identity-politics-driven party based firmly on ethnic minorities (he often delivers speeches in Spanish), the profane (he is famous for his foul mouth), and the young (given the Left's domination of college campuses and popular culture). In this way, the Democratic Party could "ride the backlash against [Trump's] presidency to revival," wrote the *New York Times.*[2]

"Despite his limited experience in electoral politics," the *Times* reported in February 2017, Perez's "calls for rebuilding the grass-roots and fostering a party that 'makes house calls again' appealed to the party insiders who have watched as the House, the Senate and finally the presidency slipped away."[3]

"We're no longer simply the committee that helps elect the president; we're the committee that helps to ensure we're electing people up and down the Democratic ticket," Perez declared.

In Perez's Democratic Party, white, blue-collar voters are out, and Latinos are in, because they are the electoral future. The strategy: enlist immigrant Latinos into the new Democratic Party, especially with the aim of tipping swing states in a Democratic direction.

Perez is a longtime resident of Takoma Park, Maryland, which has allowed noncitizen voting since 1992. With the help of politicians and "immigrant rights" groups like CASA de Maryland (Perez became its board president in 2002), noncitizen voting measures have expanded throughout the state.[4] CASA de Maryland currently operates out of a seven-million-dollar Takoma Park headquarters. The group touts itself as one of the largest immigrant advocacy organizations in the country, and has funding ties to George Soros's Open Society Foundations.[5]

In their 2012 book, *Who's Counting? How Fraudsters and Bureaucrats Put Your Vote at Risk*, authors John Fund and Hans von Spakovsky describe the new DNC chair as a hard-core progressive, obsessed with promoting unrestrained immigration to the United States. The authors noted CASA de Maryland's opposition to any enforcement of immigration laws, including pressuring local police departments not to enforce federal fugitive warrants. Perez was on the Montgomery County Council from 2002 to 2006, where he helped further CASA de Maryland's agenda. Fund and von Spakovsky documented that:

> As a councilman in Maryland in 2003, Perez sought to force local governments to accept *matricula consular* ID cards, which are issued by the Mexican and Guatemalan governments, as a valid form of identification. He insisted that individuals with such cards not have to show any U.S.-issued documents to prove their identities, even though matricula ID cards are known to be rife with fraud. No major bank in Mexico accepts them if someone tries to open an account.[6]

From 2004 to 2005 Perez was Montgomery County Council president.[7] He lost a bid to become Maryland's state attorney general in 2006 despite experience serving as a legal advisor to Senator Ted Kennedy and as a civil rights lawyer in the Clinton administration. After the election, however, he was tapped to serve as state

Secretary of Labor under then-Democratic governor, and 2016 Democratic presidential candidate, Martin O'Malley.[8]

In 2009, Obama hired Perez to work under Eric Holder in the Department of Justice Civil Rights Division. Almost immediately, controversy erupted when the Civil Rights Division decided to drop charges against two members of the New Black Panther Party after they were caught on video intimidating voters at a Philadelphia polling station. Both of the Black Panthers wore long black trench coats, jackboots, and military-style berets. One wielded a nightstick; the other, amazingly, was a poll worker.

The *Washington Post* reported, "The Obama administration months later dismissed most of the case, even though the Panthers had not contested the charges."[9] Perez told the U.S. Commission on Civil Rights that the decision not to pursue the Black Panther case was made without consulting the Department of Justice's political leadership, although an Inspector General's report later found otherwise.[10]

Throughout his career, Perez has seemed more a political partisan than a disinterested enforcer of civil rights laws, and this is especially true when it comes to voting rights. The organization he previously ran, CASA de Maryland, continued to push for noncitizen voting in that state, with the cities of Hyattsville and Mount Rainier enacting such policies in 2017, joining other cities which had previously passed similar laws. Unlike other states, Maryland permits its local municipalities to decide who can vote in local elections. According to ThinkProgress, a left-wing activist organization, Gustavo Torres, executive director of CASA de Maryland, declared the College Park city council's four to three vote to allow noncitizens to vote in elections as "a courageous step in the right direction" that "fosters inclusiveness."[11]

Not everyone agreed. "The feedback that I've gotten from my residents in District 4 has been almost overwhelming against the proposed change in our charter," City Councilwoman Mary C.

Cook told the *New York Times* prior to the council vote. The *Times* noted that Cook's husband and brother are both naturalized U.S. citizens.[12]

Speaking to Fox News when College Park, Maryland, considered a noncitizen voting measure, Ira Mehlman, spokesman for the Federation for American Immigration Reform, called noncitizen voting an "assault on the whole concept of citizenship and what it means."[13]

"If anybody who just wanders in has the same right—and an equal right—on how this country is run, then, essentially the whole concept of the nation becomes meaningless," Mehlman said.

Despite getting four of seven votes, the noncitizen voting measure actually failed to allow noncitizens to vote in College Park. The city charter required a supermajority of six votes to pass amendments like the voting measure. The city's mayor admitted "considerable embarrassment" for the oversight on the noncitizen measure in that city.[14] Still, the momentum for the effort in Maryland is clear.

Attempts to preempt such measures from spreading statewide in Maryland have failed in the Democratic-controlled Maryland Legislature. "If Osama bin Laden was alive today and he moved to Takoma Park, he could register to vote and hold office," said Republican Delegate Patrick L. McDonough of Baltimore County. "That's how ridiculous the system is." The legislature further rejected his bill that would have prohibited noncitizens from voting in Maryland elections.[15]

After the February 2017 announcement that Tom Perez would be the new chairman of the DNC, Gustavo Torres of CASA de Maryland proudly said in a video interview that community organizers across the country were coordinating "a big meeting with Tom."[16]

"We are in charge of the party," Torres continued. "We are going to mobilize our community, be engaged, and bring progressive issues that we believe are important and will change America—these values that Tom Perez has. We are very excited about this. Remember, Tom was our board president!"

When Perez arrived at the DNC, the Party's fundraising was struggling because of the strong partisan divide between the Sanders socialist wing of the Party and the Clinton left-liberal wing.[17] But Perez has received plenty of help from Democratic leaders who agree with him that the Party's future is tied to Hispanic voters.

According to the *Hill*, an anonymous DNC source said in July 2017 that former president Obama has regular contact with Perez.[18] "Hey man, it's only the future of the world in your hands," Obama reportedly joked with Perez in one conversation. David Simas, a former Obama political advisor and now CEO of the Obama Foundation, also admitted to a string of calls offering "strategic advice" to DNC officials on behalf of the former president, the *Hill* noted.[19]

It all comes down to votes. The Latino vote rose from nine million in 2008 to eleven million in 2012, with clear majorities going to Obama (67 percent[20] and 71 percent[21] respectively). In 2016, nearly thirteen million Latinos voted for president[22]—a record turnout—with 66 percent of Hispanic voters casting ballots for Hillary Clinton.[23] Yet record Hispanic turnout wasn't enough for her to win (or even match her husband's 72 percent of the Latino vote in 1996).[24] Perez's answer to that conundrum—get more Hispanic voters.

In an opinion article published by NBC News prior to Perez's DNC chairmanship, author Stephen A. Nuño expressed the new electoral strategy succinctly. "There's a faulty argument that Democrats need to bridge the gap with disaffected white working-class voters in post-industrial America and focus on making concessions to them," Nuño wrote. "If the next leader of the Democratic Party lurches Right to regain white working-class voters, they would bleed support from the fastest growing demographic in the country, one that could reshape and energize the party for decades to come."[25]

More pointedly, University of Southern California Professor Manuel Pastor made clear whom Latinos should be rooting for politically. "Every electoral season brings the high hope that this will be the year when Latinos will finally make a difference," Pastor wrote in The *American Prospect*. "The term 'sleeping giant' gets bandied around, with the hope that the wake-up occurs and that the results will be overwhelming for the good guys."[26]

Pastor added, "Applications for naturalization in the first half of 2016—which had historically been enough lead time to ensure citizenship and registration by November—were up about 30 percent above the first half of 2015." The Obama administration spent $19 million to fund its "Task Force on New Americans," chaired by Cecilia Muñoz, a former vice president of La Raza. The task force was charged with expanding services such as civics education and instruction for prospective new citizens, speeding the process for immigrants from the border to the voting booth.

Many Americans reject the idea that people should vote according to their race or ethnicity. But the cynics in the Democratic Party are betting that demography is destiny.

A common liberal view is that Donald Trump's election represented "the last gasp" of "white America." As political science professor David Cohen put it, "The demographics of the country are changing, and they're changing in favor of the Democratic Party. The election of Donald Trump is the last gasp of the white guy in American politics. It was an anomaly election."[27]

But after losing the White House to Donald Trump, and both houses of Congress, the Democratic Party's need to turn out minority voters has never been more important. Consider this post-2016 election analysis from the Huffington Post:

> Democrats may try to assure themselves that things are not so bleak. The party still pulls in nearly 90 percent of the black vote, two-thirds of Hispanic or Asian votes,

and majorities among racial and ethnic 'others.' They continue to capture a majority of women and young people. While the exit polls show that Republicans have been consistently chipping away at this coalition, the trend does not suggest the GOP will actually win majorities from any of these groups anytime soon.

But here's the rub: Republicans actually don't need to outright win—or even come close to winning—any of these demographic categories in order to come out ahead. If minority turnout is low, Republicans win. If Democrats fail to capture 2012 levels of black, Hispanic and Asian votes, they lose. It doesn't really matter if lost votes go to Republicans or independents—the outcome is the same.[28]

One approach is to create more voters. Providing amnesty to millions of undocumented immigrants, "chain migration" to bring their relatives to the United States, protecting them from enforcement of immigration laws, and a host of other compelling incentives are the way to clear electoral majorities. These policies also create a clear distinction from the Republican Party's emphasis on the rule of law, reducing immigration, and generally opposing amnesty. And if future votes are the goal, Democrats are seeding already fertile ground.

According to Pew Research, two-thirds of Hispanic voters identify or lean toward the Democratic Party.[29] In 2016, that meant 64 percent of registered Hispanic voters self-identified or leaned Democratic, while only 24 percent identified or leaned Republican. Pew also reported that the United States Hispanic population is at an all-time high at 57.5 million people, and is "the principal driver of U.S. demographic growth, accounting for half of the national population growth since 2000."[30]

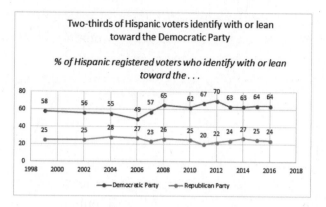

Courtesy of the Government Accountability Institute and Pew Research Center.[31]

Also from Pew: Hispanics are 18 percent of the United States population and are the nation's second largest racial or ethnic group, behind whites. At 35.7 million, Hispanics of Mexican origin are by far the largest group, with Puerto Ricans a distant second at 5.3 million. California has the largest Hispanic population of any state at 15.2 million—a 39 percent increase since 2000.[32]

Author Mark Steyn underscores the political impact of the trend by zeroing in on California. "According to the Census, in 1970 the 'Non-Hispanic White' population of California was 78 percent," Steyn notes. "By the 2010 census, it was 40 percent. Over the same period, the 10 percent Hispanic population quadrupled and caught up with whites."[33] The political demographics of the state changed dramatically, and it swung from "Reagan Country," and a Republican lock in presidential elections (from 1952 through 1988, with the exception of 1964) to one of the most liberal Democratic states in the Union. In California today, Republicans hold no statewide offices, have not had a Republican U.S. senator since 1992, nor enjoyed a majority in either house of the state legislature since 1996. California's political transformation is the model for what the Democrats would like to achieve nationally. The 2020 Census promises to show an even more pronounced demographic shift there.

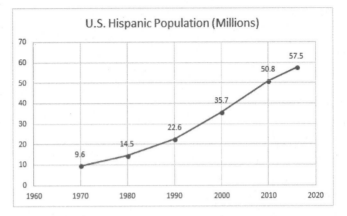

Courtesy of the Government Accountability Institute and Pew Research Center.[34]

There are an estimated 11.3 million undocumented immigrants on the electoral sidelines, about 73 percent of whom are Hispanic (and mostly Mexican).[35] The Democrats see legalized noncitizen voting, and a quicker pathway to citizenship, as vital to their electoral prospects.

The impact could potentially put presidential elections permanently out of reach for Republicans. President Trump won the Electoral College by winning the previously "blue states" of Michigan, Pennsylvania, and Wisconsin by razor-thin margins, 0.2, 0.7, and 0.8 percentage points, respectively (10,704; 46,765; and 22,177 votes).[36] Trump won Florida, a must-win for a Republican presidential candidate, by just 1.3 percent of the vote. Perez and his backers know this. It's why their strategy includes expanding voting rights for noncitizens as rapidly as possible.

The Massachusetts cities of Amherst, Brookline, Cambridge, and Newton have all passed noncitizen voting measures, even though Massachusetts state laws prohibit the cities from implementing their voting ordinances.[37] Noncitizens in San Francisco, including illegal immigrants, were given the right to vote in school board elections in early 2018.[38] That's likely to expand as noncitizen voting gains more widespread acceptance.

Under Mayor Bill de Blasio, New York City's progressive city council has been trying to legalize voting for its estimated 1.3 million noncitizen city residents.[39] In 2015, the city began issuing more than one million municipal ID cards, mostly to illegal immigrants, as an alternative to government documents such as driver's licenses or American passports.[40] Over the Trump administration's objections, city officials ordered the destruction of all personal information associated with undocumented aliens applying for municipal ID cards. A state supreme court judge upheld New York's actions.[41]

In December 2017, Democratic Mayor Rahm Emanuel of Chicago, who was previously President Obama's White House chief of staff, borrowed the idea and announced that his city will issue 100,000 new ID cards ostensibly for those having trouble obtaining state-issued driver's licenses, such as illegal immigrants. Anyone who obtains a Chicago ID will be able to use it to register to vote in the sanctuary city.

"Emanuel budgeted about $1 million this year and another $1 million in 2018 toward the program as he seeks to bolster his standing in the city's Hispanic community ahead of a 2019 re-election run," the *Chicago Tribune* reported.[42]

Both initiatives aim to counter Trump administration immigration enforcement policies. City Hall leaders have pledged to discard any personal information an applicant might present when obtaining a city ID, which can include foreign passports or "dozens of other documents."

Although federal courts have afforded states and municipalities some leeway in setting policies regarding noncitizen voting with respect to their own elections, it's clear that only United States citizens may vote in federal elections.

Ironically, the main reason both legal and illegal noncitizens cannot currently vote in federal elections, including presidential elections, is because of the Illegal Immigration Reform and Immigrant Responsibility Act of 1996, a law signed by President Bill Clinton—the spouse of the Democratic Party's 2016 candidate. This law makes it a crime, with few exceptions, for noncitizens to vote "for the office of President, Vice President, Presidential elector, Member of the Senate, Member of the House of Representatives, [or] Delegate from the District of Columbia."[43]

The law also established enforcement policies that the new Democratic Party largely rejects. In April 2016, the influential liberal news website Vox blasted the 1996 law and blamed the country's current immigration problems on the bipartisan legislation. "The immigration reform Hillary Clinton wants could be limited—or even undermined—by a law her husband signed," the article's subtitle says.[44] The same month, thirty-two progressive Democrats signed a congressional resolution condemning the law.[45]

As noncitizen "voting rights" measures continue to spread across the country, it will be up to Democratic-controlled cities, such as New York City, San Francisco, Chicago, and Takoma Park, Maryland (home of Tom Perez) to self-police against noncitizen voter fraud in federal elections while they simultaneously allow noncitizen voting in their own elections.

This seems unlikely, considering 53 percent of Democrats believe illegal immigrants should be allowed to vote in any election, according to a 2015 Rasmussen poll.[46] Voters under the age of forty were twice as likely to favor illegal immigrant voting, according to the survey. Meanwhile, DNC chair Perez declared that there is a greater chance of being fatally struck by lightning than witnessing voter fraud.[47] Note that this talking point was also stated by the

Brennan Center, which, like Perez's previous and current employers, takes millions in Soros funding.

The minimization of the threat and impact of voter fraud is vital to defending the argument that our elections are currently problem-free, and that any efforts to increase their security are racially motivated. It's a defense Eric Holder's Department of Justice made often, including in the highest court of the country.

In June 2013, the United States Supreme Court struck down a provision of the 1965 Voting Rights Act that barred states with a history of discrimination from making any changes to their voting procedures unless granted permission to do so by the federal government. Permission, called "preclearance," would have needed to be granted by Holder himself, who proudly embraced the label of an "activist" attorney general.[48]

Legal analyst Jeffrey Toobin explained that the court, which ruled five to four in the decision known as *Shelby County vs. Holder*, found that "times have changed so much that the formula [for deciding which states are more prone to discriminate] is invalid."[49]

Holder disagreed, arguing that the nine states, including Alabama, Texas, Mississippi, and Alaska, as well as certain counties in California, New York, and Florida, would return to discriminatory practices if that provision from the half-century-old law were struck down. Holder's assumption was that any changes in voter ID laws or other acts to strengthen the integrity of the voting process would be discriminatory.

When the state of Ohio removed inactive voters from its rolls ahead of the 2016 election, it faced challenges from the Ohio Chapter of the A. Philip Randolph Institute and the Northeast Ohio Coalition for the Homeless, represented by the ACLU. Ohio scrubbed inactive voters who did not respond to letters attempting to confirm their address under the reasoning that non-respondents were no longer eligible voters in the state. After a U.S. District Court upheld the legality of the policy, the Holder's Justice Department joined with the plaintiffs in appealing the case to the Sixth Circuit, which then declared the practice unconstitutional.[50]

Maintaining accurate state voter rolls is a requirement under the National Voter Registration Act (the so-called Motor Voter law), an act of Congress signed into law by President Bill Clinton in 1993. The Obama Department of Justice departed from both Clinton and Bush administration interpretations of the law.

The Trump administration is taking a different approach. Under new Attorney General Jeff Sessions, the Department of Justice reversed its position from the previous administration and supported a Texas law requiring voters to register with a driver's license or similar ID.[51] It likewise backed Ohio's voter roll purges, filing an amicus brief with the U.S. Supreme Court in support of the Ohio effort. But while the new position reflected the stance of Sessions and those directly under him, it was not the position of many within the Justice Department's Civil Rights Division, which handles voter rights cases.

The Trump Administration's amicus brief in support of the Ohio law, unlike its Obama administration predecessor, was not signed by career Civil Rights Division lawyers. According to Justin Levitt, the former Department of Justice deputy assistant attorney general overseeing voting rights cases in the Obama administration, that was no accident. "It's a signal…It says this was a political decision that did not have the buy-in of the people who are the keel of the Justice Department."[52]

But then, the position of veterans of the Obama Justice Department, including Levitt, was clear. And it wasn't exactly nonpartisan. Before he joined the Obama administration, Levitt had worked for the Brennan Center. There, he wrote the Center's oft-cited 2007 report titled "The Truth about Voter Fraud." What was Levitt's version of the "truth?"

"On closer examination," he wrote, "many of the claims of voter fraud amount to a great deal of smoke without much fire. The allegations simply do not pan out."[53]

Ten years later, the Trump administration launched a bipartisan voting commission, officially known as the Presidential Advisory Commission on Election Integrity. While much of the media focused on President Trump's assertion that three million illegal votes were cast in the 2016 presidential election, the commission was asked to study voter registration and voting processes in every state, and recommend improvements to the American system of elections.[54] Integral to its mission was conducting a review of state voter rolls, but the commission finally had to disband, because of states refusing to comply and under the weight of legal actions by well-funded opponents, again including the Brennan Center.[55] Some groups filed legal challenges even before the commission's first meeting. It appeared that many groups, including the Brennan Center, had no interest in allowing a bipartisan federal commission to examine the integrity of state voter rolls. One can wonder why, but one really doesn't have to wonder much. Under the Obama administration, the Department of Justice had worked to undermine measures that guarded against voter fraud.

According to Robert Knight, senior fellow for the American Civil Rights Union, a nonprofit legal organization founded by a former Reagan administration official, AG Holder had little interest in maintaining the integrity of American elections. Holder appointed Richard C. Pilger to head the Election Crimes Branch in the Public Integrity Section of the Criminal Division of the Department of Justice. Pilger was put in charge of prosecuting voter fraud and campaign financing offenses. Despite years of evidence of voter fraud from across the country—noncitizen voting, felon voting, deceased individuals voting, double-voting, and more—his branch prosecuted a mere *three* cases of fraud involving egregious vote-buying schemes between 2010 and 2015 (the most recent data available).[56]

Despite the new, very different administration now in office, Pilger remains in his job, and other alumni of the Obama-era Civil Rights Division continue to fight against voter ID laws and against investigating voter fraud. As for Perez, the 2018 midterm elections will be the first opportunity to see if the constituency he pursues as DNC Chair and the electoral conditions he allowed as assistant attorney general combine for success at the ballot box.

George Soros—the Man behind the Ballot Booth

ver wonder why voter ID laws and other election integrity initiatives are called "voter suppression" laws, "voting restrictions," and "anti-voting rights" measures? And why lawsuits seem to pop-up all over the country just as soon as elected representatives pass them? Public opinion couldn't be any more opposed to such efforts.

Voter ID laws generally have widespread public support. For example, in August 2016, Gallup found that four out of five Americans supported voter identification laws. The finding included 95 percent of Republicans, 83 percent of Independents, and 63 percent of Democrats.[1]

When the issue was coupled with early voting, Gallup found even stronger support.

"Though many of the arguments for early voting and against voter ID laws frequently cite minorities' voting access, nonwhites' views of the two policies don't differ markedly from those of whites. Seventy-seven percent of nonwhites favor both policies, while whites favor each at 81 percent," the Gallup survey said.[2]

The result was not an outlier. Other election year polls show similar support.

A Fox News poll in 2014 found that 70 percent of registered voters favored voter ID laws to combat voter fraud at the ballot box. Majorities of every major demographic group, including African Americans and Democrats, supported voter ID laws.[3]

In 2012, a *Washington Post* poll showed nearly the same results. Almost 75 percent of Americans believe people should have to show photo ID to vote. About half of those polled saw voter fraud as a "major problem" in presidential elections.[4]

"Moreover, big majorities of those whom critics see as bearing the brunt of the laws are supportive of them, including about three-quarters of seniors and those with household incomes under $50,000 and two-thirds of non-whites," the *Post* reported.

A 2012 *Atlanta Journal-Constitution* review of Georgia's voter ID law found that voter participation among African Americans and Hispanics has increased dramatically since the law's passage.[5] The law was adopted in 2005, survived a court challenge in 2007, and was in place for the 2008 presidential election.

Prior to the law's adoption, voters were able to present a utility bill as one of seventeen forms of permitted identification. The new law required Georgia voters to show a valid identification with a photo on it, including a passport or military or student ID.

Despite racially charged critiques (the attorney general would refer to voter ID laws as "poll taxes"), turnout among the purported victims of voter suppression actually skyrocketed after the law's implementation.

"Elections data reviewed by the *AJC* show that participation among black voters rose by 44 percent from 2006—before the law was implemented—to 2010," the *AJC* reported. Among Hispanics, the increase for the same period was 67 percent. Turnout among whites rose 12 percent."[6]

Alabama also has a voter ID law, and in its special election to fill the open seat held by longtime Republican Senator Jeff Sessions in December 2017, record African American turnout helped elect the Democratic candidate. The *New York Times* gingerly faced the election's outcome in an article headlined, "Black Turnout in Alabama Complicates Debate on Voting Laws."[7]

The fact is common sense voter ID laws having nothing to do with "voter suppression" or "voting restrictions." The Left invokes these phrases, which hearken back to the era of segregation, only for their emotive effect. The real issue is something else entirely; it is a concerted effort by the activist Left to win elections by bringing thousands if not millions of noncitizens to the polls, and in doing so, create an environment in which voter fraud can flourish.

There is a large, well-funded, and well-coordinated network of groups dedicated to undermining election integrity laws and initiatives wherever they are being considered, and virtually all the tentacles lead to the controversial progressive billionaire, George Soros, and his global social justice organization, the Open Society Foundations (OSF). Recently leaked documents from Open Society Foundations' servers show just how far-reaching and deeply engaged the Soros network is in shaping American elections.

In August 2016, a hacker group, DCLeaks, posted online more than 2,500 OSF documents, dating back to 2008. Cyber security analysts believe DCLeaks was tied to Russian meddling in the 2016 U.S. election.[8] The authenticity of the files has not been disputed, as with the hacked emails of the Democratic National Committee and Hillary Clinton campaign chair John Podesta. The files expose OSF's breathtaking plans to influence European elections, dictate American foreign policy, sway U.S. Supreme Court decisions, and even target domestic interest groups that support American election integrity reforms.[9]

One document describes funding efforts to turn the "text and history of the Constitution into a progressive sword."[10] Another document outlines a three-part electoral strategy of "litigation, legislation and local mobilization." Another document proudly claims success for blocking the implementation of election reform laws in Pennsylvania, Florida, Ohio, Texas, Wisconsin, and South Carolina. Other documents refer to grantees such as the League of Women Voters, the NAACP, and the ACLU, which often sue states and localities, and, most recently, the Presidential Advisory Commission on Election Integrity. Media Matters for America, a staunchly progressive media watchdog group, was mentioned as having received hundreds of thousands of dollars to monitor Spanish-language media. Known for pressuring news organizations to cover left-wing issues and causes, Media Matters shared office space with John Podesta's Center for American Progress, a progressive think tank that also received millions of dollars of Soros support.

The documents also show references to the intentional development of "narratives," "new frames and language," and "research-informed messaging," meant to shift the national conversation about voting laws to the political Left, by using a pliant news media.

One document marked "Voting Narrative in the Media" brags about the impact of the groups' various efforts. "From September until the election, grantees found over 300 examples of the new voting messaging used verbatim in media outlets, including the *New York Times*, *Philadelphia Inquirer*, the Huffington Post, and Politico," the document reads. "Grantees are currently tallying the full coverage of voting issues in the media this fall. Media attention access reached levels unseen in prior election years."

The point cannot be emphasized enough—there is nothing like this effort anywhere else on the American political spectrum.

Soros has dedicated tens of billions of dollars towards his political objectives and has built a vast complex of organizations and individuals to do his bidding. Funding for Open Society Foundations' U.S. programs reaches hundreds of different grantees.[11]

After the eighty-seven-year-old Soros transferred $18 billion of his personal wealth to OSF in October 2017, Darren Walker, president of the mega-philanthropy Ford Foundation, put the organization in perspective for a friendly *New York Times* profile.

"There is no foundation in the world, including the Ford Foundation, that has had more impact around the world than the Open Society Foundations in the last two decades," Walker said. "Because there is no part of the world that they have not been. Their footprint is deeper, wider and more impactful than any other social justice foundation in the world."[12]

But Soros's main focus is the United States.

To that end, he has coupled his left-wing political ideology and significant financial interests with those of the Democratic Party. As the *New York Times* went on to explain, Soros spent many millions of dollars supporting Hillary Clinton in 2016: "Mr. Soros eventually became one of the biggest donors to Democrats, including Mrs. Clinton. During the last election cycle, Mr. Soros gave millions to super PACs that opposed Mr. Trump and supported other Democratic candidates and causes. He also bet big in the markets that Mr. Trump would lose the election, a wager that cost him about $1 billion."[13]

It was hardly Soros's first foray into American elections. In 2004, Soros poured millions left-wing activist into groups—like ACORN, ACT, and UnidosUS (formerly La Raza)—whose get-out-the-vote efforts were of questionable legality. ACT and ACORN were sanctioned and fined by the Federal Elections Commission after the 2004 election, with ACORN nailed for filling out voter registration cards with fake names, including former boxing champ Leon Spinks.[14]

Who is George Soros, exactly?

According to GeorgeSoros.com, the official website for biographical information about the multi-billionaire hedge fund investor, he is one of the world's foremost philanthropists—a fabulously wealthy do-gooder. He financially supports individuals and organizations across the globe that fight for freedom, transparency, justice, and equality. Who could be against that?

"My success in the financial markets has given me a greater degree of independence than most other people," he's quoted as saying.[15] The website notes "that independence has allowed him to forge his own path towards a world that's more open, more just, and more equitable for all."

OSF says Soros has given more than $32 billion of his personal fortune to his organization since founding it in 1979, with the funding focused on "those who face discrimination purely for who they are."[16]

Soros was born György Schwartz in Hungary in 1930. He survived the Nazi's occupation of Hungary only to see Communists take over in 1947. He then fled Hungary for England, where he attended the London School of Economics. In 1956, he immigrated to the United States and entered the world of high finance, becoming one of the richest men in the world.

Now nearly ninety years old, Soros continues to take an active interest in the OSF's work. He travels widely to push its social and political objectives, and personally lobbies for policy changes with world leaders. The OSF website proudly claims that the one consistent thread throughout his legacy is his "commitment to fighting the world's most intractable problems."

But at best, that's only half the story.

Soros is also a convicted felon. Despite his vast wealth and global influence, his lawyers failed to convince the highest court in France to vacate a 1988 conviction for insider trading. Soros was caught buying and selling 95,000 shares of Société Générale, a Paris-based multinational bank after receiving information of a planned corporate raid.[17]

In 1992, Soros pocketed $1.5 billion in a single month when, as a hedge fund investor, he leveraged a ruthless short-selling position against the British pound. The currency crashed, and British taxpayers lost nearly $4.5 billion in what became known as "Black Wednesday." The media dubbed Soros "The man who broke the Bank of England," while "retirees on fixed incomes saw their pensions diminished and their savings wiped out," according to Stefan Kanfer, of the Manhattan Institute's *City Journal*.[18]

Apparently those poor and working-class retirees fell outside the scope of Soros's service for a world that would be "more equitable for all."

Even liberal firebrand and Nobel Prize-winning economist Paul Krugman condemned Soros's toxic effects on financial markets. The billionaire financier spawned another kind of movement—one of cruel market speculation. "[N]obody who has read a business magazine in the last few years can be unaware that these days there really are investors who not only move money in anticipation of a currency crisis, but actually do their best to trigger that crisis for fun and profit," wrote Krugman in 1999. "These new actors on the scene do not yet have a standard name; my proposed term is 'Soroi.'"[19]

Soros is indeed a man of contradictions: He's an über-capitalist and a social justice demigod. His financial headquarters is in Curaçao, a poor Caribbean island nation that serves as an international tax haven for the super-wealthy. His Open Society Foundations was ironically rated one of the least open, or transparent, think tanks in the world in 2016.[20] A self-proclaimed friend of the poor, Soros ranked as Forbes's twentieth richest person in the world (before his $18 billion gift to OSF).

Soros, who is Jewish, has also taken strong positions against Israel by supporting groups that urge boycotts, sanctions, and disinvestment from companies doing business with it. He pushes open-borders immigration policies in Europe and the United States and is a major backer of movements to legalize marijuana. Though a U.S. citizen, he spent at least $550,000 to undermine "Brexit," after the British people voted to leave the European Union (while still managing to profit from Brexit).[21] And he is a primary supporter of the network of groups trying to undermine the integrity of American elections.

In 2004, Soros poured millions into 2004 a new political player, a tax-exempt organization called "America Coming Together (ACT)." The group, which worked almost exclusively on behalf of Democrats, was geared almost exclusively towards get-out-the-vote efforts. With yet another presidential election hanging in the balance, ACT spent over $10 million on election day on forty-five thousand paid canvassers, along with another twenty-five thousand volunteers.

One of the states ACT targeted in 2004 was Minnesota. Traditionally a blue state, Minnesota was a concern for Democrats in Senator John Kerry's campaign because Al Gore had carried it in 2000 by only 2.5 percent, and with only 48 percent of the total vote. Minnesota also features a unique vulnerability in its voting rules: a person can register to vote on election day in Minnesota without any identification, so long as a fellow voter "vouches" for their residence and address.

Enter ACT. Ahead of election day, ACT bragged its members would knock on five hundred thousand doors in Minnesota alone, and state residents would receive in-person visits from ACT members two or three times, along with numerous mailers.

In an internal email written weeks before the November election, they also communicated about their plan to take advantage of Minnesota's same-day registration and vouching rule. ACT officials told email recipients, "Election Day is upon us. You are confirmed to volunteer with ACT....We will be creating name badges that include your Ward and Precinct information for each of the thousands of volunteers that day to make it easier to find a volunteer to vouch for a voter at the polls."[22]

This email is a key piece of evidence in any argument about the relevance and prevalence of voter fraud. It not only shows the open flouting of the intent of already vulnerable election laws, but it also shows *the coordinated political effort to do so.*

The 2004 election wasn't the only time, and Minnesota wasn't the only place where Soros-backed groups tried to ram as many questionable voters through voting precinct loopholes. ACT would end up paying $775,000 in fines for violating campaign finance laws. It was disbanded in 2005. But Soros did not give up. And he definitely did not go away.

A later tactic in Soros's efforts to influence elections involved putting like-minded people in charge of state elections. Each state has a chief elections officer who has ultimate authority over elections in the state. In most cases, the official is the secretary of state. Some of them are appointed, but most are elected. And Soros and company zeroed in on the office with a political action committee called the Secretary of State Project (SOSP) that works to elect Democratic secretaries of state.

SOSP helped elect five Democratic secretaries of state in 2006, spending $500,000 and losing just two of seven races.[23] All told, SOSP backed eleven winning candidates in states such as Ohio, Nevada, Iowa, New Mexico, and Minnesota.

The group disbanded after 2012, though another group with less obvious Soros ties has since emerged with a similar aim.

The Soros network is active in the courts too.

A Soros-funded lawyer by the name of Marc Elias, or as the *Washington Post* refers to him, "a Democratic super lawyer with multimillion-dollar backing," has been suing to block election integrity measures across the country.[24]

Soros has reportedly given at least $5 million to a trust that bankrolls Elias's litigation efforts to block voting laws that, he argues, limit the impact of important Democratic Party constituencies.

Michael Vachon, Soros's spokesman, told the *Post* that Elias approached them with proposals to "challenge state (voting) restrictions," and promised his efforts would help Democratic candidates "up and down the ballot."[25]

Elias is no ordinary lawyer. He is a partner at the prestigious law firm Perkins Coie LLP. The firm has a huge presence in Washington, D.C., and represents almost the entire upper strata of the Democratic Party, including the Democratic National Committee (DNC), the Democratic Senatorial Campaign Committee (DSCC), the Democratic Congressional Campaign Committee (DCCC), the Democratic Governors Association (DGA), the Democratic Legislative Campaign Committee (DLCC), the House Majority PAC, the Senate Majority PAC, Priorities USA, Emily's List, more than forty Democratic senators, and more than one hundred Democratic House members.[26]

Perkins Coie was also centrally involved in the infamous Trump "dossier" that led to a Foreign Intelligence Surveillance Act (FISA) warrant authorizing the surveillance of employees of the Trump campaign and White House transition team.[27]

It was Elias and Perkins Coie that retained Fusion GPS, an opposition research firm, on behalf of the Hillary Clinton campaign and the DNC from April 2016 until just a few days before the presidential election. The timeline overlaps an extended period of Elias's litigation war against voting integrity laws across key swing states, including Ohio, Virginia, and Wisconsin.

The coordination of interests is troubling. From the outside, it appears a Soros-funded lawyer, who was also the general counsel for Hillary Clinton, a Soros-backed candidate for president, was simultaneously suing to block election laws with the intention of benefiting Clinton's electoral prospects, and by extension, Soros's political and financial prospects.

But the official line seems more like a distinction without a difference: Elias was admittedly paid by George Soros to sue

certain states ahead of the 2016 election, but was said to be working independently on behalf of Perkins Coie, while conveniently
receiving the public endorsement of the Clinton campaign for his
voting lawsuits.[28]

It's as if the Soros-funded lawsuits had nothing to do with the
Soros-backed candidate, for whom Elias worked. Still, whether
directly or indirectly, Soros and the Clinton campaign tried to
block voter ID laws meant to combat voter fraud.

Elias's lawsuit in Ohio came with some embarrassment. One
of his clients, Ohio Organizing Collaborative, claimed that the
state's ID law amounted to "voter suppression." But the Ohio
Organizing Collaborative was itself later investigated for election
crimes. One of its paid canvassers pleaded guilty to thirteen felony
counts of voter fraud, including registering dead people.[29]

In May 2016, a U.S. District Court upheld Virginia's voter ID
law, which requires voters to show photo identification at the
polls. The lawsuit was brought by the Democratic Party of Virginia, represented by Marc Elias (Perkins Coie had already filed
a pair of redistricting suits against the state by that time). A federal judge dismissed the suit and noted that the IDs required by
the law are free in Virginia, thereby imposing no financial hard-
ship. The judge added that none of the witnesses called by the
plaintiff had been denied the ability to vote. So despite arguing
against a law many believe is a common-sense response to potential fraud, Elias's suit claiming voter suppression couldn't find any
suppressed voters."

"I guess George Soros isn't done wasting his money yet," a
spokesman for Virginia's House Speaker told the Virginia *Daily
Press,* about the ruling. "Which is disappointing, because he's got
a lot more of it than the taxpayers who are stuck paying to defend
the Democrats' politically motivated lawsuit."[30]

Virginia's Attorney General Mark Herring, also a Democrat,
refused his constitutional obligation to defend the state's law, and

instead hired a Republican-leaning law firm to defend the state's voter ID law in court.

Herring was elected in 2013 by a mere 165 votes out of 2.2 million total votes cast, and not without controversy. A 2017 investigation by the Public Interest Legal Foundation found that thousands of undocumented noncitizens were registered to vote in the state, and many cast ballots over a period of years.[31] "Virginia election officials routinely fail to alert law enforcement about these illegal votes or registrations," the Public Interest Legal Foundation report found.

Elias and his Democratic Party clients vowed to appeal the federal court's ruling on Virginia's voter ID law. They demanded that a higher court take the case "as quickly as possible." But a U.S. Court of Appeals refused until after the 2016 presidential election, and upheld the prior ruling in favor of the integrity law. For Soros and his team, the political ploy didn't work.

But the scorched-earth litigation strategy can still yield results, even without victory in the courts. In a section of a leaked internal report marked "Voting Narrative in the Courts," the Open Society Foundations document explains how, win or lose, the aims of high-profile litigation can be amplified through the media, where public opinion is often shaped. "OSF funding also ensured legal groups could achieve tremendous success in the courts this year, blocking or blunting every voting law that was challenged before the election," the report states. The report also boasted that, despite losses in court, the movement was winning in the media. "The intense media coverage and the resonance of the new messaging had a real and direct impact," the document said. "For example, the ruling on the South Carolina photo ID case echoed the new messaging."[32]

Some of the grantee organizations mentioned in the leaked OSF documents are ostensibly nonpartisan—such as the League of Women Voters, the American Civil Liberties Union, and the NAACP Legal Defense and Educational Fund—but they also file lawsuits aligning with OSF's political views. All three organizations, or their local chapters, for example, sued to block the work of the bipartisan presidential commission on election integrity in 2017. George Soros's son, Jonathan (an OSF board member), and former Attorney General Eric Holder both sit on the board of the NAACP Legal Defense and Educational Fund. The organization's president, Sherrilyn Ifill, is the former head of the Open Society Foundation's U.S. Programs division, which oversees and funds OSF's American election activities.[33]

Common Cause, the Electronic Privacy Information Center (EPIC), and the Brennan Center for Justice, all have funding ties to the Open Society Foundations, and helped sue the now-disbanded election integrity commission into oblivion. EPIC lost its lawsuit in federal court in December 2017, but vowed to continue tying up the commission by immediately filing an appeal.[34]

The Brennan Center is in many ways OSF's go-to organization when it comes to fighting election reforms and communicating with the news media. The Brennan Center was listed in the leaked OSF documents as one of several groups receiving more than $500,000 annually from the Open Society Foundations, along with the Leadership Conference on Civil and Human Rights, the Center on Budget and Policy Priorities, the Center for American Progress, the Advancement Project, and the Center for Community Change. According to publicly available grant records, The Brennan Center received $3.2 million from OSF in the election year 2016.

In July 2017, the Government Accountability Institute (GAI), a nonprofit led by journalist and author Peter Schweizer, released a report on double-voting fraud. Days after the release of the report, former Brennan Center attorney Justin Levitt contacted Ken Block of Simpatico Software Systems. Block was GAI's data consultant on the double-voting project. He said in an interview that Levitt had tried to persuade him to turn over his data without fully identifying his intentions. Block refused. Levitt also used to work in the Civil Rights Division of the Obama Justice Department, which had previously been led by current DNC Chair Tom Perez.

Block added that no one should rely on Levitt's much-quoted 2007 Brennan Center report on "The Truth About Voter Fraud." That report, Block explained, "pre-dates centralized electronic databases." Block noted that the Brennan Center analysis would be insufficient if it hadn't mined actual voter data. "It's an emotional conclusion, not scientific. It would be like the Securities and Exchange Commission snooping around trading floors, and only looking for suspicious characters."

Block, on the other hand, took a rigorous, data-driven approach to identify fraud in the GAI report. With high statistical confidence, Block determined there were thousands of illegal double-votes and thousands more troubling voter irregularities.[35] "You have to look at data," Block emphasized. The fact that so few of the groups that deny widespread voter fraud do so, is telling, in Block's opinion. Block suspects it's because they would rather "not determine whether voter fraud exists."

Other election-related groups and funding arms that were referenced in the leaked OSF documents include the Constitutional Accountability Center, the Roosevelt Institute, the National Council of La Raza, the State Engagement Initiative, the Black Civic Engagement Initiative, the Democracy and Power Fund, and Project Vote. The Democracy Alliance is also referenced. Democracy Alliance is a partnership alliance and includes a coalition of activist groups, including the Climate Fund, the Democracy Fund, the Inclusive Economy Fund, the Latino Engagement Fund, the Black Civic Engagement and Action Fund, and the Youth Engagement Fund—all of which feature their own funding sources and electoral objectives.

Numerous references are made in the leaked documents about the Soros network's intentions to manipulate the news media. Also mentioned are intricate efforts to develop news-ready narratives for media consumption, often in consultation with professional public relations and research firms. One of the most impressive references was to some three hundred OSF grantees reporting verbatim "new voting messaging" across major news media outlets.

In the wake of the 2013 *Shelby County v. Holder* case, in which the U.S. Supreme Court struck down two provisions of the Voting Rights Act of 1965 as inconsistent with current voting realities, the Soros network waged a public relations war, with the help of a friendly media, to try to paint this as a setback for civil rights.

The media is friendly to Soros not just because of a shared ideological bias or agenda, but because of money. The Media Research Institute estimates that since 2003, "Soros has spent more than $48 million funding media properties, including the infrastructure of news—journalism schools, investigative journalism, and even industry organizations."[36]

Even if influencing the media might be considered par for the course for activist special interest groups, less excusable is punishing Americans for whistle-blowing on voter fraud—and Soros-backed groups have tried to do just that. Just ask Catherine Engelbrecht.

In many ways, Engelbrecht and her husband Bryan are a classic American success story. A successful small business woman, Engelbrecht and her husband have built an oil-field machine shop. She was an active PTA mom and a founding member of a church in Houston, Texas. She was also active in volunteer work, and never thought much about politics.

Unfortunately, that didn't stop powerful political forces from taking an interest in her after she volunteered to be a poll watcher. She witnessed voter fraud and blew the whistle on it. Instead of being rewarded for her vigilant efforts to protect democracy, her life was turned upside down.

The Internal Revenue Service, the Federal Bureau of Investigation, the Bureau of Alcohol, Tobacco, and Firearms, and even the

Occupational Safety and Health Administration, all took aim at Engelbrecht—a private citizen—in an apparently coordinated effort to intimidate her into silence and crush a grassroots election integrity movement before it could spread any further.

Engelbrecht did not back down.

"I am an average American who, prior to 2009, had never been active in the processes of government; but, after volunteering to work at the polls in Texas in the 2009 elections, I saw fundamental procedural problems that I felt could not go unaddressed," she told the House Committee on Oversight and Government Reform in 2014.[37]

"So, I started True the Vote, an organization that grew into a national movement to ensure that every American voter has an opportunity to participate in elections that are free and fair," she testified.

Engelbrecht was part of a small group of volunteer poll workers who reported witnessing "blatant, undeniable acts of election fraud," as well as an alarming lack of trained election workers.[38] She founded True the Vote, a nonprofit organization dedicated to education, research, and support for poll volunteers, centered on the belief that "election integrity is an issue that should unite us, not divide us."[39] But True the Vote's commitment to speaking out about the "misleading messaging of those who insist voter fraud does not exist" was enough to attract the ire of the Open Society Foundations' powerful political machine. Leaked documents show that OSF saw True the Vote as a threat to its highly partisan election objectives.

A web of OSF-funded organizations targeted True the Vote.

The Campaign Legal Center took the lead, the leaked documents show. "CLC (Campaign Legal Center) is focusing most of its efforts on the threat posed by private 'challenger' groups and, to that end, has been gathering information on the activities of such groups, including Houston-based True the Vote."

The Campaign Legal Center lists the Open Society Foundations as one of its institutional donors, and George Soros's son, Jonathan, an OSF global board member, as an individual donor. (Soros's son himself is a prominent billionaire donor to Democratic and liberal causes.)[40] The Brennan Center for Justice, a recipient of millions of dollars in Soros funding, also donates to the Campaign Legal Center, as does OSF-funded Project Vote, and the Soros-backed Tides Foundation.[41]

Creating "narratives" is a recurring theme in the OSF documents, and the goal here was to "frame" election integrity reforms as "voter restrictions" or "voter suppression," and to submit such a narrative to the Department of Justice, then-headed by Attorney General Eric Holder, as a way to cast True the Vote in a bad light.

"Working in partnership with Transparency Fund grantee Project Vote, CLC has pieced together a narrative that strongly suggests a widespread effort by True the Vote to suppress minority voting," the leaked documents say. "CLC made Open Records Requests to officials in Houston to obtain all communications between True the Vote and Houston election offices, obtained and analyzed these documents and presented their findings to the United States Department of Justice last month."

Engelbrecht's on-the-record congressional testimony in February 2014 detailed how the Obama administration, the Department of Justice, the IRS, and progressive political activists set out to target and destroy her merely for doing her civic duty.

"In nearly two decades of running our small business, my husband and I never dealt with any government agency outside of filing our annual tax returns. We had never been audited, we had never been investigated. But all that changed upon submitting applications for the non-profit statuses of True the Vote and King Street Patriots," she said.[42] "Since that filing in 2010, my private businesses, my nonprofit organizations, and family have been subjected to more than 15 instances of audit or inquiry by federal agencies." She added:

- In 2011, my personal and business tax returns were audited by the Internal Revenue Service, each audit going back for a number of years.
- In 2012, my business was subjected to inspection by OSHA, on a select occasion when neither my husband nor I were present, and though the agency wrote that it found nothing serious or significant, it still issued fines in excess of $20,000.
- In 2012 and again in 2013 the Bureau of Alcohol, Tobacco, and Firearms conducted comprehensive audits at my place [of] business.
- Beginning in 2010, the FBI contacted my nonprofit organization on six separate occasions wanting to cull through membership manifests in conjunction with domestic terrorism cases. They eventually dropped all matters and have now redacted nearly all my files.[43]

Engelbrecht also testified that the IRS wanted every Facebook and Twitter post she'd ever made, information about possible political aspirations, names of every group to whom she'd ever presented election integrity materials, and the groups and locations where she planned to speak in the future.

During her testimony, she even called out the House Oversight Committee's ranking member, Democrat Elijah Cummings of Maryland, citing his participation in the abuse. "Three times, Representative Elijah Cummings sent letters to True the Vote, demanding much of the same information the IRS had requested," Engelbrecht testified. "Hours after sending the letters, he would appear on cable news and publicly defame me and my organization."[44]

One of those letters, dated October 4, 2012, accused her of waging a "campaign to challenge legal voters."[45]

Cummings responded by saying that there is no one "who cares more about the rights of citizens" than he does.

"Just as you all have the passion, and I respect that, I have the passion to make sure that no one—Tea Party, Republicans, or Democrats—no one is blocked from voting," he said. "I will fight until I die for the right to vote."[46]

Once again, an effort to protect the sanctity of American elections produced veiled references to racist motivations.

Cummings mentioned that his eighty-eight-year-old mother once did not have the right to vote because of racial discrimination, and that he did not want her "to pass away with the thought that people are losing their right to vote."

Engelbrecht maintained that True the Vote and other election integrity organizations exist for the very purpose of protecting the sanctity of elections, and the rights of legal voters.

In his October 4 letter, Cummings accused True the Vote of engaging in a "criminal conspiracy."[47] The accusation, made by a high-ranking elected official against a private citizen, and issued as a press release, was repeated across media outlets without evidence. Former Federal Elections commissioner Hans von Spakovsky blasted the idea of criminal wrongdoing. "True the Vote's efforts to identify the registrations of illegal aliens, dead voters, and individuals registered in more than one state have no such intent and can't have any such effect," he said. "In truth, True the Vote stands accused of doing the work that election officials ought to be doing themselves but all too often don't."[48]

The IRS has since admitted to mistreating True the Vote and other groups it regarded as conservative or affiliated with the Tea Party, saying in October 2017—after much congressional pressure, and condemnation from Attorney General Jeff Sessions, who said "There is no excuse for this conduct"—that it "expresses its sincere apology" for "heightened scrutiny and inordinate delays," and for demanding unnecessary information from private citizens.[49] The IRS settled two separate class action lawsuits involving nearly five hundred groups as a result of its admitted abusive activities.

In January 2018, U.S. District Judge Reggie Walton issued a consent decree acknowledging Engelbrecht's First Amendment rights had been violated by the federal government.[50] The ruling stated that "discrimination on the basis of political viewpoint in administering the United States tax code violates fundamental First Amendment Rights."

Today, True the Vote is a national volunteer organization with members in all fifty states, and its election integrity work continues to grow. It offers a range of education materials and training tools for volunteer poll workers, and it has created an online means of reviewing county voter registries for anyone across the country to report possible inaccuracies or fraudulent records. That effort alone has led state and county governments to take steps to maintain more accurate voter rolls. With the help of Bush-era Department of Justice Civil Rights Division attorneys, True the Vote's accountability efforts have led to successful legal actions in Florida, Ohio, and Indiana.

"After all the things that have been done to my organizations, to my family, and to me, many people would have quit," Engelbrecht told House lawmakers. "Many Americans have quit. I have heard, over and over, that people are afraid to tell their stories because of what has or might happen to them and their families at the hands of our own government.

"I will not surrender. I refuse to be intimidated. I will not ask for permission to exercise my Constitutional rights," she said.[51]

Engelbrecht has vowed to fight on. But so has Soros.

What's next seems to be something called the 2020 Project. The year 2020, of course, is a presidential election year. The leaked

OSF documents show the Soros network is planning to be in full political activist mode.

"The 2020 Project is intended to connect the interests of nearly all programs, from voting rights to immigrant political engagement," an internal strategy document says, adding that "the project will feature significant consultation and engagement with our anchor and core grantees, Democracy Alliance partners, and other donors, and field leaders, such as Planned Parenthood, progressive labor, and other allies."[52]

Since 2015, the OSF funding arm known as U.S. Programs has been targeting a small number of "red" states, including Arizona, Georgia, and North Carolina, with the intention of creating "a national impact." But 2020 isn't just a presidential election year, it's also when the Census Bureau will undertake its decennial population count, upon which congressional redistricting depends. Documents from OSF show that redistricting is a priority for their organizations, as is including undocumented immigrants in the Census. In early 2018, the Trump administration announced the inclusion of a question about citizenship status on the 2020 Census, drawing a lawsuit on behalf of seventeen states, including New York, Pennsylvania, Virginia, and Illinois.[53]

The project is set to run through 2022, when the first elections under new congressional district boundaries would occur. "The year 2020 reflects the convergence year for the Census, presidential, congressional, and legislative elections, and redistricting, forming a 'North Star' around which U.S. Programs and Open Society Policy Center could organize and assess its work."

Soros's groups understand the importance of 2020. The real question is: do the American people, who overwhelmingly want honest elections, know what is at stake? And are they aware of the size, scope and sophistication of the network actively working to subvert their interests?

We've Been Here Before:
A Brief History of Voter Fraud

Not surprisingly, voter fraud has been a part of American elections since colonial times, when elections were social occasions and voters often expected free liquor and food from candidates seeking their votes.

Who participated in such behavior? Two future presidents, as it turns out.

In 1755, a young George Washington lost his first campaign for a seat in the House of Burgesses largely because he did not provide alcohol at the polls. Three years later, he plied voters with beer, whiskey, rum punch, and wine, and won.[1] Thomas Jefferson also followed this strategy, which favored wealthy men who could lay on greater hospitality.[2]

The Virginia House of Burgesses, however, later passed a law making it illegal for any candidate or any person on his behalf to provide "money, meat, drink, entertainment or provision....in order to get elected." The penalty was disqualification.

Another way to swing votes to one's side was to engage in what was called in colonial times "faggot voting." Voting was then reserved to predominantly white landowners. To create more friendly voters for their chosen candidate, these landowners would give deeds to landless men, who would return the deeds after voting. The lack of a secret ballot ensured that the "faggot" complied with the landowner's wishes.

In 1760, the Rhode Island colony tried to address the problem of "faggot voting" by providing power to the Assembly to review the names of freeholders and to disqualify anyone whose landownership was questionable.[3]

Due to the lack of formal rules addressing voting procedures, the local sheriff was often charged with supervising elections and could, if so motivated, influence their outcome in any number of ways. Whether by choosing polling locations and their hours of operation, or sometimes merely by outright fraud, local sheriffs could simply pick the candidate they wanted and declare him the winner.[4]

After declaring independence on July 4, 1776, each former colony set out to construct a state constitution, and a number of states sought to reform their voting procedures.

Some states abolished religious tests for voting and some granted voting rights to all taxpaying, free, adult males. As early as 1777, Vermont became the first state to grant universal manhood suffrage. New Jersey permitted women to vote in substantial numbers for the first time in American history (thanks to an apparently accidental phrase in the new state constitution).[5]

Even with the adoption of the U.S. Constitution in 1787, "there were still no federal laws regarding who could vote. The decision fell to states with many maintaining the standard that favored white men of property, wealth, and education."[6]

At the beginning of the nineteenth century, Massachusetts enacted the first registration law in the United States. In Massachusetts, the "assessors of every town or plantation were required to prepare lists of qualified electors, and in the towns these lists were submitted to the selectmen, posted, and revised prior to each election. To make those revisions, the selectmen or assessors met on the day of the election immediately preceding the voting to hear applications for registration."[7]

But voter registration remained the exception prior to the Civil War. Early registration systems were rarely comprehensive and were originally created by local government officials. These officials were responsible for compiling the names of those eligible to vote in their jurisdiction, usually based on their personal knowledge or on information learned by going door to door. With a few notable exceptions, it was only toward the end of the century that most states began enacting statutes that "shifted the burden of establishing eligibility from the state to the individual."[8]

Earlier moves to require voter registration led to a debate over residency requirements. In 1857, a proposal in Iowa to require a three-month county residency requirement met resistance. A similar effort to require a six-month residency requirement failed in Maryland.[9]

With new laws and regulations, legal challenges materialized.

In 1832, a Massachusetts man was denied the right to vote because his name was not on the list of voters that the city had drawn up per a previous law. He challenged in court and lost, with the court ruling that as long as the voter had the right to verify his registration, the existence of a voter registration system did not interfere with the right to vote. The case, which became known as *Capen* v. *Foster*, was the first legal challenge of voter eligibility in Massachusetts history.[10]

It would certainly not be the last. But in addition to legal challenges, the new election laws enacted during the late eighteenth and nineteenth centuries also led to some creative, even colorful, new schemes of voting fraud.

There were, for instance, "colonizers"—groups of voters who were paid to move into certain wards before an election to ensure the outcome. There were "floaters"—voters who sold their votes to the highest bidder. And there were the "repeaters"—who famously voted "early and often," sometimes abetted by disguise.[11]

There was old-fashioned voter intimidation, too, including "cooping," in which innocent bystanders were grabbed off the street by so-called "cooping gangs" or "election gangs" working on the payroll of a political candidate. These captive voters would be kept in a room, called the "coop," and given alcoholic beverages to make them agree to cast votes (often as disguised "repeaters," wearing wigs, fake beards, and moustaches, and different clothes) for the election gang's candidate. If they refused to cooperate, they would be beaten or even killed. Many of the cooping victims were immigrants, and in cities where immigrant voters were viewed as a threat, cooping could also involve keeping these voters captive until the election was over.[12]

As the nation expanded westward, so did disputes over elections. On November 29, 1854, the first election in the Kansas Territory was held and Democrat John Whitfield was selected as the territory's first delegate to Congress. The election of Whitfield, who was a pro-slavery settler, was immediately contested by Free Staters, who claimed that thousands of pro-slavery voters from Missouri had snuck into the territory to cast votes.

Even though the total number of ballots cast in that election exceeded the total number of eligible voters, Kansas Territorial Governor Andrew Reeder approved the election to avoid continued violence.

Voter fraud in Kansas resumed, however, when on March 30, 1855, it held an election for its first Territorial Legislature.

Once again, slavery was an issue and, once again, voters from Missouri crossed into the territory to cast votes, resulting in thirty-seven of thirty-nine seats in the legislature being won by pro-slavery candidates. Governor Reeder invalidated the results and ordered a special election, which still left the pro-slavery contingent holding twenty-nine seats.

This election was also disputed. Amid rising tension in the territory, Congress sent a special committee to Kansas in 1856. The committee report concluded that if the election on March 30, 1855, had been limited to "actual settlers" it would have elected a Free-State legislature. The report also determined that the currently seated legislature "was an illegally constituted body, and had no power to pass valid laws." [13]

Nevertheless, the pro-slavery territorial legislature convened in its new capital of Pawnee on July 2, 1855. "The legislature immediately invalidated the results from the special election in May and seated the pro-slavery delegates elected in March. After only one week in Pawnee, the legislature moved the territorial capital to the Shawnee Mission on the Missouri border, where it reconvened and passed laws favorable to slavery."[14]

Slavery remained a divisive issue in different ways after the Civil War, as former Confederate states, now occupied by Union forces and under martial law, were gradually eased back into the Union under policies of Reconstruction that granted voting rights to African Americans but also left bitter resentment among many white Southerners who thought their own rights had been trampled.

Reconstruction ended in South Carolina in 1877. In 1880 a congressional election pitted incumbent Democrat John Richardson against Republican and former slave Samuel J. Lee. Darlington County, South Carolina, overwhelmingly black, was a key voting bloc in the election. In a previous election, Darlington County had voted 80 percent Republican, but the 1880 vote went more than 90 percent Democratic.

This massive voter shift raised inevitable suspicions, and on December 15, 1880, Lee sent Richardson a notice specifying twenty points of challenge, including ballot box stuffing and reports of multiple violent incidents of voter intimidation.

What followed was a two-year-long federal investigation into this race and eighteen other contested elections. The House Committee on Elections, chaired by Republican Representative William H. Calkins of Indiana, eventually ruled that in South Carolina's First District "fraud, violence, and intimidation were practiced and fraudulent returns were made, which must be corrected.[15]

Such corruption was hardly limited to the West and the South; in fact the big city political machines of the East and Midwest were among the most notorious, including New York City's Tammany Hall.

During the latter half of the nineteenth century, Tammany Hall, a group of Democratic Party political fixers, turned voter fraud into a simple art, handing out pre-marked ballots and watching carefully as they were cast, making special use of immigrants who were quickly introduced to the Tammany way of voting. In 1868, the *Nation* reported that Tammany Hall had set up a "naturalization mill," instantly certifying newly arrived immigrants as citizens, and enrolling them as Tammany voters.

Tammany was so efficient at election-fixing that between 1868 and 1871, the votes cast in the city totaled eight percent more than the entire voting population voting—"the dead filling in for the sick," as one contemporary wag put it.[16]

New York City's corruption, severe as it was, was far from unique.

In Baltimore, for instance, vote-fixing could get even uglier: a notorious Whig Party organization called the "Fourth Ward Club" hired thugs to seize innocent strangers and foreigners, drug them with bad whiskey and opiates, and send them out to cast multiple votes.

Political scientists estimate that in many urban areas fixers routinely manipulated 10 to 15 percent of the vote.

A 1929 study by the Brookings Institution, looking back on U.S. elections in the nineteenth century, observed that "indifference, fraud, corruption, and violence have marked the operation of our electoral system."[17]

The corruption extended to national politics as well. Both major parties stole votes with abandon in the 1876 presidential election contest between Republican Rutherford B. Hayes of Ohio and Democrat Samuel Tilden of New York. That race ended in a deadlock, resolved only after a congressional commission delivered the presidency to Hayes by a single, disputed electoral vote. The next three presidential elections (resulting in victories for Republican James Garfield, Democrat Grover Cleveland, and Republican Benjamin Harrison) proved so close that fraud may have played a role in their outcomes, too.[18]

With corruption rampant, reform was inevitable. Disputed congressional, state, or local elections were often appealed to Congress, state legislatures, or the courts. Increasingly, legislative bodies set up committees to adjudicate disputes among rival candidates.[19]

The most significant reform adopted during this period addressed how ballots were created, distributed, and collected. It was common practice for partisan newspapers to print filled-out ballots, which party workers distributed on Election Day for voters to drop directly into the ballot boxes. Poll monitors could easily see who voted for whom, which allowed political machines to threaten or intimidate dissident voters. That changed, however, in the last two decades of the nineteenth century, when states moved to secret ballots—popularly known as "Australian ballots," which are official ballots, printed by the government, and cast privately at the polling place.

In 1888, the city of Louisville adopted the secret ballot as part of a backlash against corruption and electoral fraud. The measure spread quickly to other states, spearheaded by Progressive reformers scandalized by how party machines controlled elections—especially in urban areas teeming with new immigrants.[20]

Most states began moving to secret ballots for statewide and national elections soon after the presidential contest of 1884. Kentucky was the last state to do so in 1891, though not all states had government printed ballots. Georgia, for instance, did not have government printed ballots until 1922 and South Carolina did not until 1950.[21] While the new secret ballot system promised fairer elections, it did not take long for power-hungry operatives to find new tricks. Fraud efforts moved from political machines operating on the streets to governmental authorities responsible for running elections.

Just seventeen years after Louisville became the first city to adopt the secret ballot, the results of the city's 1905 municipal election were overturned by a 4–2 vote of the Court of Appeals. The court ordered the removal of an entire city government even after the incumbent administration had served in office for over a year.[22]

The new ballots and voter registration rules made it more difficult to employ the use of "repeaters" in Louisville. But it did not address problems with manipulating who registered to vote. Election Day fraud began with registration day fraud. Someone registered illegally could then vote "legally." It's a problem that continues to plague American elections today.

Papers in nearby St. Louis warned Louisville citizens that eighty "practical politicians" were repeatedly registering under false names. The paper sarcastically noted that the repeaters "would work wonders increasing the population of Louisville." By padding the rolls with thousands of illegal voters, the city machine was now prepared to "get out the vote" in November. A quarter of the city's poll workers in the 1905 election had a vested interest in the outcome, as they were either city or county employees or had relatives who worked for the government. Another 13 percent of the poll monitors were listed as "gamblers" or "bartenders." [23]

And during the post-election investigation, a careful review of Louisville's voter rolls revealed 1,829 known illegal registrations, of which 793 had voted in the mayoral election.[24]

Still, strict reforms such as the requirement to register before Election Day, did clean up some of the fraud, and, in some cases, caused voter "turnout" to fall precipitously. Historians Gary Cox and Morgan Krause noted that turnout in New York State elections dropped some 15 percent after the anti-fraud measures took effect.[25]

In a noteworthy case in 1910, a reformist judge in Adams County, Indiana, brought to trial and convicted 1,690 voters—or 26 percent of the whole electorate—for selling their votes.[26]

The earliest reliable studies of election fraud in the 1920s and 1930s found that individual voters almost never committed fraud on their own. Conspiracies by politicians or election officials were behind most violations.[27] The twentieth century saw the rise of new political machines, all of them Democratic. Powerful politicians, like Huey Long in Louisiana and Lyndon B. Johnson in Texas were adept at using local political officials to deliver desired results in specific counties.

There were also big-city machines like the Curley machine in Boston, the Hague machine in Jersey City, and the Daley machine in Chicago which not only controlled city politics but could deliver their cities' voters in state and national elections. Their means of influence and control were manifold, but could be as simple as manipulating the names on voter rolls or printing their own unofficial ballots and distributing them ahead of election day. Therefore, when voters turned up at the polls, the party leaders could keep track of who was voting the "right way" by checking the color of the unofficial ballots they previously distributed.

Johnson, who had lost a Texas Senate race due to fraud early in his career, never complained about the process. Instead, he copied the practice and marched to victory in a disputed election in 1948. According to reports, Johnson won by just eighty-seven votes out of almost one million cast after recruiting supporters to stuff ballot boxes in a poor county in the Rio Grande Valley. According to Johnson biographer Robert Caro, the deciding votes were all written with the same pen and the same hand.[28]

Another future president arguably almost saw his career derailed due to fraudulent voters.

In 1962, a new district was added to the Georgia Senate, drawing the attention of a local peanut farmer named Jimmy Carter. Carter narrowly lost the primary but challenged the results in court, citing, among other issues, dead and imprisoned voters who were listed on the rolls. After a drawn-out legal battle, the court ordered a recount, handing Carter the victory just three days before the general election, which he would win by fewer than a thousand votes.

One would like to think that such ballot shenanigans were part of America's colorful past. But electoral fraud remains a serious issue. In 1994, for example, a federal judge invalidated a Pennsylvania state senate election, decried "a massive scheme" by Democrats abusing the use of absentee ballots to steal the seat, and ordered the seat filled by the Republican candidate.

Arlene C. Rubin, executive director of Project LEAP (Legal Elections in All Precincts), a Chicago-based organization that monitors elections, believes that abuse of absentee ballots has moved voter fraud "out of the polling places and into people's living rooms."[29]

The abuse of absentee ballots was also crucial in determining the winner of a congressional election in California in 1994. That year, a Republican candidate named Loretta Brixey lost a close race for the Anaheim City Council in California. Undeterred,

Brixey got creative in her next political effort. She reverted to her maiden name and changed her political affiliation, running for Congress the following year as Loretta Sanchez, and as a Democrat.

Challenging incumbent Republican Congressman Bob Dornan was a difficult task in GOP-leaning Orange County, so Sanchez relied heavily on courting the district's growing Latino population.

Sanchez won the race by a mere 979 votes. Dornan contested the election result, alleging that illegal voting had occurred. Dornan was correct, a House committee later ruled.

California officials threw out as invalid nearly 150 absentee ballots and the House committee determined that hundreds of noncitizens had voted in the election. House investigators flagged 4,700 questionable voter registration affidavits, but chose not to pursue them. That decision was fateful, since Sanchez officially prevailed in the recount by just thirty-five votes.

And it was a consequential victory. Changing demographics in the district, the power of incumbency, and perhaps lax policing of the voter rolls helped Sanchez hold that seat for the next twenty years. Bob Dornan, her predecessor, had been a stalwart conservative Republican. According to the *Washington Post*, the former Republican Loretta Sanchez voted with Nancy Pelosi 98 percent of the time.[30]

While election fraud might be less overt than in the past, and while the power of Democratic Party machines might have dwindled, there are still many ways to try to subvert honest elections— the most obvious being the manipulation of voter rolls, blocking voter ID laws, and opening up voting to noncitizens.

The demise of big city Democratic political machines has given way to progressive, nonprofit groups funded by wealthy individuals that influence the voting process under the mission of expanding democracy. However, as you will see, this mission is more about political power than ensuring the right to vote for all eligible citizens.

Ironically, the increasing use of absentee ballots in modern elections has recreated problems that were prevalent before secret ballots were adopted during the end of the nineteenth century. The use of secret ballots, filled out in government sanctioned offices on election day, was adopted to prevent voter intimidation. The ubiquitous use of absentee ballots moves the voting process out of government offices into living rooms, neighborhoods, community centers, and even churches.

The rise in the influence of non-profit groups on the electoral process and the increasing use of absentee ballots, both raise questions about the ability for election supervisors to maintain the integrity of elections by ensuring each vote that is cast is from an eligible voter.

CHAPTER

4

The American Dream—the Problem with Noncitizen Voting

One of the largest and most concerning ways voter fraud can affect American elections is when noncitizens vote. Federal law explicitly states that only U.S. citizens can vote in federal elections, but ineligible noncitizens vote all the time. The only question is how much. Estimates vary, but there's no denying the incidents of voter fraud and voter registration fraud—both felonies—occurring throughout the country.

Almost a year after the 2016 presidential election, police in Tewksbury, Massachusetts, arrested Joel Santiago-Vazquez, a resident of Lawrence, Massachusetts, for drug dealing. Undercover detectives arrested him with sixteen grams of cocaine and crack, hidden in a Pringles can with a false bottom. Santiago-Vasquez had a Massachusetts driver's license, a vehicle registered in his name, *and was registered to vote, but was not a U.S. citizen.*

Boston's WFXT-TV station, a Fox affiliate, investigated the incident by cross-referencing several dozen other local criminal suspects facing deportation proceedings against voter databases. After "checking just a few dozen names of criminal defendants facing deportations against voter databases," the station discovered three other noncitizens registered to vote, "making it highly likely that many more noncitizens are among the nearly 36,000 registered voters in Lawrence."[1] Lawrence's mayor, Willie Lantigua, refused to discuss the issue with Fox reporters. A little more digging revealed stories of alleged voting problems in his 2009 mayoral race.

Wayne Hayes, who worked for Lantigua's opponent in 2009, said he both witnessed and provided evidence of voter fraud to local authorities and to the Massachusetts secretary of state.

"A gentleman was seen by one of the poll workers for Abdoo's campaign walk in and vote at one table, leave, come back, switch his jacket and put on a cap and went to the other table and voted there under two different names," Hayes said.[2]

Yet, nothing was done. When Fox reporters interviewed an attorney for one of the noncitizens registered to vote, he said his client had "no recollection of ever registering or agreeing to register." He gave that answer, perhaps, because without *intent* to commit fraud, the felony becomes a "mistake."[3]

There are apparently a lot of such "mistakes" in Lawrence. Hayes claims the problem is rampant, alleging that 15 to 20 percent of the voters in Lawrence are not citizens. And the problem is hardly limited to that corner of Massachusetts.

Fifteen hundred miles away in Southwest Florida, investigative reporters from an NBC affiliate cross-checked voter rolls with a list of people who were excused from jury duty because they were not U.S. citizens. Without much effort, they quickly discovered nearly one hundred noncitizen voters, including a resident of Cape Coral who told them, "I vote every year."[4]

The news team confronted several other individuals, including a Naples woman who said she had no idea how she was registered to vote. "I mean, how am I supposed to know," she said. Curiously, public records showed she had voted six times over more than a decade.[5]

A Jamaican national told NBC2 that it wasn't his fault he was registered to vote. "It's their mistake, not mine," he said, although a copy of his voter registration application showed he indicated he was a U.S. citizen on the form. Knowingly submitting false information on a voter registration form is a violation of federal law, and a third-degree felony in Florida, punishable by up to five years in prison and a $5,000 fine. But prosecutions, much less convictions, are extremely rare.

In part this is because federal law—the National Voter Registration Act of 1993—prohibits election officials from demanding proof of citizenship when someone registers to vote, and election officials cannot initiate fraud investigations on their own. "We don't have any policing authority," Lee County, Florida, Supervisor of Elections Sharon Harrington told reporters. "We don't have any way of bouncing that information off any other database that would give us that information."[6]

The news team in Florida presented nearly a hundred names to both Lee and Collier County elections supervisors. Official letters were then sent to the individuals in question asking them to verify their citizenship status.

"It could be very serious. It could change the whole complexion of an election," Harrington concluded.[7]

Thanks to NBC2's efforts, elections offices in Lee and Collier counties now request copies of jury excusal forms indicating lack of citizenship. But that is not the policy at the federal level. Or even for any state.

Two thousand miles west, journalist Glenn Cook of the *Las Vegas Review-Journal* found similar election integrity problems in

Nevada. Cook wrote a series of reports on noncitizen voting in 2012. County election officials there typically verify the identity of an applicant registering to vote by matching his application to a driver's license (which illegal immigrants can't legally acquire in Nevada) or state-issued ID card.

Nevertheless, voter fraud can still be surprisingly easy. Third parties—like unions or get-out-the-vote groups—can submit voter registration applications without driver's license information or Social Security numbers. But unions aren't the only ones facilitating potential voter fraud.

Cook found that, at taxpayer expense, Nevada state officials "mailed post cards to an undetermined number of noncitizens, felons and deceased Nevadans inviting them to register to vote online."

When these registrations are approved they are tagged with an "ID Required" label, which means these potential voters will be asked to provide identification when they show up to vote. Under state law, however, a utility bill or a health insurance card can qualify as voter ID, though neither one would be proof of citizenship. "Strictly speaking, we do not verify citizenship," the public information officer for the Nevada DMV told Cook.[8]

But that's not all. Cook reported that he interviewed two immigrant noncitizens who were clearly not eligible to vote, but were actively registered for the 2012 general election. He said they were signed up by Culinary Local 226, a Las Vegas labor union representing food and service workers.

"They speak and understand enough English to get by. But they don't read English especially well," Cook explained. "They say the culinary union official who registered them to vote didn't tell them what they were signing and didn't ask whether they were citizens. The immigrants said they trusted that the union official's request was routine, thought nothing of it and went about their work."[9]

Later, union canvassers ordered them to vote. One of the immigrants said a union official even came to his home and threatened him with deportation if he didn't cast a ballot in the November election.

Stories like this, Cook concluded, "validated my worst fears about Nevada's weak voter registration standards and voting safeguards."

In fact, similar reports had surfaced two years before, in 2010, that the Nevada culinary union squeezed its members to vote for Democratic Senator Harry Reid against his Republican challenger Sharron Angle. *National Review* obtained emails from the Reid campaign to the executive management of Harrah's casino in which campaign officials complained that their employees weren't voting at the rate of other casinos' employees.[10] A Reid staffer said the campaign had "connected with Culinary" and pressured Harrah's executives to "put a headlock on your supervisors to get them to follow through." The campaign even offered to get Reid himself on the phone if it would help.[11]

Reid, the top Democrat in the United States Senate, would go on to win, though not without other suggestions of voter fraud. Given what Cook exposed two years later about Culinary Union election activities, it's reasonable to wonder how many noncitizen voters ended up contributing to that win.

As Cook, now the managing editor for the *Las Vegas Review-Journal*, noted, "We have an honor system that's exceedingly easy to cheat and gives political parties and politically active groups a powerful incentive to break the law without much risk of being caught."[12]

"Voter registration fraud is not a groundless conspiracy," he added. "It is not a hypothetical threat to election integrity. In Nevada, a battleground state that could decide the presidency and control of the U.S. Senate, it is real."[13]

Another problem is that election officials themselves often don't know what to do about noncitizen voter fraud, and when they do act the consequences can be unpredictable.

For instance, Rosa Maria Ortega and her mother came to the United States from Mexico as illegal immigrants. Her mother was deported when Ortega was a teenager, but she vowed to do things the right way.

"When my mom was here, she did everything illegal," Ortega, now thirty-seven, said in an interview. "I wasn't going to let that happen to me."[14]

Despite dropping out of school before high school, Ortega still made a life for herself and her four children. At eighteen, she signed up for the Jobs Corps and started working at a state employment office. She married and worked three jobs to provide for her family. She obtained her green card and permanent U.S. residency. But as she would soon learn, while those achievements bring with them many things, the right to vote is not one of them.

Proud of her permanent resident status, Ortega registered to vote in Dallas County, Texas, without challenge. She voted in five elections as a Dallas County resident, even serving as a poll worker.[15] When she moved west to neighboring Tarrant County, she registered to vote again, only this time she checked the box affirming that she was a noncitizen. When her application was rejected in March 2015, Ortega called election officials to find out why, and was told, correctly, that only citizens are eligible to vote. Ortega told Tarrant County election clerk Delores Stephens that Dallas County "did not have a problem with her" voting,[16] and filled out another application, this time stating that she was a citizen. This put Stephens in an awkward spot. Unsure what to do, Stephens queried the office of Texas secretary of state.

Stephens was told, per her later court testimony, that she was forbidden by law from questioning Ortega's status as a citizen and was therefore required to process her application.

"We weren't sure what to actually do with her," Stephens testified.

Eventually, the matter garnered the attention of the Texas attorney general's office, and Ortega was charged with voter fraud.

Ortega still doesn't understand why she was arrested.

"I thought I was doing something right," Ortega told the *New York Times*. "It wasn't to hurt somebody, or the state, or the government. I even worked for the government."

"I voted like a U.S. citizen," she said. "The only thing is, I didn't know I couldn't vote."[17]

Ortega's lawyer Clark Birdsall complained that under the law Ortega "can own property; she can serve in the military; she can get a job; she can pay taxes. But she can't vote, and she didn't know that," adding bluntly: "She has a sixth-grade education. She didn't know she wasn't legal."[18]

Ortega's lawyer claimed the attorney general's office was prepared to dismiss all charges in exchange for Ortega's testimony before the Texas Legislature on her experience of voting illegally.

But the Tarrant County district attorney rejected that deal, according to Birdsall, seeing the case as an opportunity to highlight her office's efforts to crack down on voter fraud.[19] Instead, the thirty-seven-year-old mother of four was sentenced to eight years in prison, and fined $5,000 for each of her two counts of illegal voting. She will be eligible for parole after just two years but would face immediate deportation upon the completion of her sentence.[20] In March of 2018, she was freed on bond, pending appeal of her case.[21]

Birdsall blamed the severity of Ortega's sentence on the election of Donald Trump. "Donald Trump has this country at war with one another over this illegal immigration situation," Birdsall said. "What should have been reduced to a misdemeanor or pled out has resulted in an eight-year sentence. And the ironic thing is, she voted Republican." That wasn't the only irony, because her case had nothing to do with illegal immigration or with Donald Trump, it had to do with illegal voting. Even so, the penalty certainly seemed disproportionate to the crime, at least given that in 2011 Hazel Brionne Woodard, a Democratic precinct chairwoman candidate, was arrested for having her son cast a ballot under his father's name, which was also illegal. Unlike Ortega, though, Woodard received only probation.[22]

Ortega's case made national headlines because of the severity of her sentence. But while most media stories highlighted the need for reforming our electoral laws so that noncitizens can legally vote, few mentioned that her case highlights how easy it is for noncitizens to cast illegal ballots now.

A similar case is that of Margarita Del Pilar Fitzpatrick, a Peruvian immigrant. When she applied for an Illinois driver's license, she showed a U.S. green card and Peruvian passport to the desk clerk who asked if she would also like to register to vote. Fitzpatrick hesitated. "Am I supposed to?"[23]

"It's up to you," the desk clerk told her.

Fitzgerald's daughter Connie says her mother interpreted this as meaning that she was legally allowed to register.

As with Rosa Maria Ortega, Fitzpatrick's decision to "check the box" would lead her not only to the voting booth, where she would vote twice in federal elections, but also to a deportation order.

Like Ortega, who was released on bond awaiting appeal, Fitzpatrick is fighting back.

Fitzpatrick is now hoping to have hear case heard by the U.S. Supreme Court, after an unsuccessful appeal to the Seventh Circuit.

Both Fitzpatrick and Ortega are victims of a provision in the 1993 National Voter Registration Act, which both allows people to register to vote when they apply for a driver's license and expressly forbids DMV officials from discouraging anyone from registering, even, according to Connie Fitzpatrick, "clearly ineligible folks, like my mother, who should never have been asked to register to vote in the first place."[24]

As Connie Fitzpatrick wrote in her online fundraising page, "In the end, my mother believed that the DMV official knew the law better than her and would never mislead her or offer her an opportunity to commit an unlawful act. Well, the DMV official did mislead her, and because of that she faces immediate deportation."[25]

State governments, even if inadvertently, are often complicit in voter fraud. In 2016, Vermont enacted a law that allows anyone who renews a driver's license to be automatically registered to vote. That meant, of course, that noncitizens who renewed their licenses went onto voter rolls.

Luke McHale, a Burlington resident and green card holder, received a letter saying he was now registered to vote. But he knew he shouldn't be and called the DMV. "My husband is not a citizen," his wife Becca McHale said. "We know he's not allowed to vote."[26]

An embarrassed Michael Smith, the director of operations for the Vermont DMV, said a car registration address change had triggered the automatic voter registration inappropriately. He also ordered his staff to suspend automatic registrations while they investigated other possible "glitches."

Vermont Secretary of State Jim Condos deflected the controversy, saying that "I know this is a hot-button issue these days, with what's coming out of Washington. This was an error DMV found in the system. They notified us. We immediately pulled the plug. We're moving forward to fix the system."[27] He pointed out that automatic registration, also done in Oregon, California, and West Virginia, could add between twenty thousand and forty thousand new voters to Vermont's rolls over the course of four years. Unstated was how many of those might be noncitizen voters who, unlike McHale, might not know that they are ineligible to vote.

One month before the November 2016 general election, a Pennsylvania state legislator raised alarm that not only were noncitizens registered to vote in the Keystone State, but they were actively encouraged to vote by the state government.

The problem, again, was the state's Motor Voter system.

"There's certainly the potential for hundreds, if not thousands, of foreigners here legally and illegally to be on our voter rolls, and a certain percentage who are casting ballots," said Representative Daryl Metcalfe, the Republican chairman of the House State Government Committee.[28] "We've got a lot of integrity issues that need to be addressed," he said.

Metcalfe was proven right in 2017, when Pennsylvania's chief elections officer resigned after revelations of voter fraud in Philadelphia, a city not unfamiliar with unusual voting patterns. In 2012, for example, fifty-nine city precincts somehow failed to record a single vote for Republican Mitt Romney.[29]

Larry Sabato, a political scientist with the University of Virginia, noted the statistical improbability of a major presidential candidate receiving literally no votes. "I'd be surprised if there weren't a handful of precincts that didn't cast a vote for Romney. But the number of zero precincts in Philadelphia deserves examination," he said. "Not a single vote for Romney or even an error? That's worth looking into."[30]

Prior to the 2012 elections, City Commissioner Al Schmidt, the lone Republican on the Philadelphia City Commission, released a twenty-four-page report titled "Voter Irregularities" that highlighted confirmed incidents of voter fraud along with recommendations on how to prevent it. One of the points it addressed was noncitizen voting.[31]

"In 2012 alone, the Philadelphia Voter Registration Office has cancelled the registrations of 19 illegally registered voters in Philadelphia County who are not U.S. citizens," the city-funded report stated, noting that seven of those individuals had voted in multiple elections over the previous decade.

Finding nineteen illegal registrations may seem insignificant, but the report was not meant to be a comprehensive study of voter fraud; it was only to confirm that noncitizen voting is among the many types of fraud that do occur. Seen against the backdrop of nearly non-existent voter registration verifications, its implications are still dramatic.

The report recommended that city election officials work with U.S. Citizenship and Immigration Services (USCIS) to develop a better method for identifying noncitizen voter registrations in Philadelphia County. "The current method—waiting for USCIS to notify the Voter Registration Office once an individual has applied for citizenship—is clearly inadequate," the report concluded. In other words, registered noncitizens who don't apply for citizenship will remain on the rolls unchallenged.

Pennsylvania voters must declare on their voter registration applications that they are U.S. citizens. It's as easy as checking a box. Once the application is signed, the citizenship declaration and other pertinent information such as name and address are considered a legal affidavit. But there's no follow-up to make sure the citizenship information is correct.

The applicant's self-declared eligibility "is the only measure taken to verify citizenship prior to a voter registration application being processed by the Voter Registration Office," the report states. Relying on this de facto "honor system," Schmidt's report determined, has resulted in "some non-citizens" registering and participating in Philadelphia elections.

Fast forward to 2017, and nothing appears to have changed.

As part of a review of the 2016 election results, Commissioner Schmidt announced "hundreds" of ineligible noncitizens were registered to vote in Philadelphia, with nearly half casting general election ballots they shouldn't have.[32] That number would soon balloon to 1,160 illegal registrations statewide, according to the Pennsylvania Department of State.[33]

Likely, the real number is far greater. Most of the noncitizen registrations came to light because the individuals in question self-reported, not because of any oversight function by the Pennsylvania Department of State. This is why the state's chief elections officer, Pennsylvania Secretary of State Pedro Cortés, resigned, abruptly and without comment.

On October 11, 2017, Pennsylvania's Democrat Governor Tom Wolf announced Cortés's departure in a 349-word "personnel update" email to media, with no explanation. Officially, there was nothing to discuss. Subsequent emails, however, revealed Wolf had fired Cortés.[34]

Cortés, a registered Democrat, had previously served as secretary of state under another Democrat governor, Ed Rendell, a longtime Clinton ally and ardent supporter of Hillary Clinton's 2016 presidential campaign.

In the months leading up to the 2016 election, Cortés's office sent 2.5 million notices to licensed drivers who were not registered to vote. These notices encouraged recipients to register in time for the upcoming presidential election. The problem was that not everyone receiving the notices was a U.S. citizen, and Cortés knew it.

Pennsylvania—like most states—allows documented noncitizens to obtain a driver's license. (Twelve states, including California, allow *illegal* immigrants to obtain a driver's license.) If these legal noncitizens register to vote when they obtain their driver's licenses, as permitted by federal Motor Voter laws, there's almost no way to identify and remove them from the voter rolls short of their stepping forward and saying they made a mistake.

Cortés admitted to a Pennsylvania legislative committee in early October 2016 that several resident noncitizens had contacted the secretary of state's office to say they weren't eligible to vote; the husband of one noncitizen woman testified that his wife received a notice, but never followed up. She had apparently been automatically registered by the district's election office.[35]

According to Logan Churchwell, a spokesman for the voter-integrity group True the Vote, the reason Cortés sent out the notices was because he had to. It was a condition of joining the Electronic Registration Information Center, a multi-state partnership with the express mission of improving the accuracy of state voter rolls. ERIC includes about twenty states and the District of Columbia.

ERIC began as a Pew Charitable Trusts project and was seeded with funding from the MacArthur Foundation, the Joyce Foundation, and George Soros's Open Society Foundations. Leaked OSF documents say that ERIC grant awards are "based on the number of mailings that each state is obligated to send to unregistered residents."[36] But Pennsylvania State Representative Daryl Metcalfe told an interviewer that "neither ERIC nor state officials ever told legislators that sending notices to non-voters would be a condition of joining the consortium."[37]

One week before Cortés' abrupt resignation, Metcalfe and fifteen of his legislative colleagues sent the secretary a letter "to express our dire concerns" about the potential for fraud with the system of registering voters when they applied for or renewed their driver's licenses.

"Cortés knew this was an issue," Metcalfe said afterwards. "It is interesting that his resignation occurred within a week of our letter to him about this serious issue," he told the *Philadelphia Inquirer*.[38]

"We were hoping to hold [a hearing] to get answers that are important to Pennsylvania voters about how these foreign nationals have gotten onto voter rolls," Metcalfe said.[39]

Metcalfe did, in fact, hold a hearing on noncitizen voting on October 25, 2017. While the media focused its coverage on the tiny percentage of ballots known to be cast illegally, it ignored the far bigger point made by Linda A. Kerns, who testified at the hearing. "So, we now know that noncitizens have registered to vote and have voted in Philadelphia elections. We also know that, absent self-reporting of this crime, authorities have few tools to correct these illegalities which affect every voter in Philadelphia who properly registers and votes and, in a Commonwealth-wide election, affects properly registered voters outside Philadelphia. Their votes are diluted."[40]

Also testifying was Noel H. Johnson of the Public Interest Legal Foundation (PILF), a national non-profit group focused on election integrity. PILF had produced its own report documenting how illegal immigrants voted in past Philadelphia elections. The report found that city officials did nothing to prevent or remove not just noncitizen registrations, but also those of thousands of ineligible felons. Johnson said that local election officials "don't even think it's a problem."[41]

PILF's efforts to investigate further were stymied by state officials who refused to allow PILF access to its public voter roll data. In February 2018, PILF filed a federal lawsuit alleging as many as one hundred thousand noncitizen voters are illegally registered in Pennsylvania—each one representing a potential felony.[42]

PILF found similar voter registration problems in New Jersey and in the Commonwealth of Virginia. In a sample of just eight Virginia counties, it found 1,046 noncitizens registered to vote illegally.[43] If that number seems small, consider that the election of the state's top law enforcement officer, who would ultimately be tasked with prosecuting cases of voter fraud, was decided by a number much smaller than that.

In 2013, Democrat Mark Herring defeated Republican Mark Obenshain in Virginia's attorney general race by well under a thousand votes. Virginia has had many close races in recent years. In local races, the margins of victory can be even thinner. In 2014 a state senate seat was won by nine votes, and in 2017 a state delegate seat was awarded by drawing lots after a tied vote. A few illegally cast votes can easily determine an election.

Given the findings of PILF's follow-up report which documented 7,474 ballots cast by voters elections officials would remove for citizenship status, one wonders how many other races were swung because of voter fraud.

Illegal Immigrants and Identity Theft

Some of these votes were undoubtedly cast inadvertently by noncitizens who did not realize they were ineligible to vote. In fact, voter fraud deniers often cite the lack of incentive for noncitizens to vote, given the risks of deportation or damage the act can do to the hope of obtaining citizenship. The fraud of an illegal vote is often accompanied and even motivated by another type of fraud—one that no one denies. But like voter fraud, the problem of illegal immigrants acquiring fraudulent Social Security numbers is also not a top law enforcement priority.

In April 2016, then–IRS Commissioner John Koskinen stunned members of the Senate Finance committee by telling them that the IRS essentially ignores illegal immigrant identity theft, because it is "in everybody's interest" to have illegal aliens "pay the taxes they owe."[44] and the IRS does not contact the Department of Homeland Security or anyone else about this fraud, because, in typical bureaucratic style, the IRS does not consider that its job.

Senator Dan Coats of Indiana summed up Koskinen's testimony by saying: "What we learned is that…the IRS continues to process tax returns with false W-2 information and issue refunds as if they were routine tax returns, and say that's not really our job [to police identity theft]. We also learned that IRS ignores notifications from the Social Security Administration that a name does not match a Social Security number, and you use your own system to determine whether a number is valid."[45]

According to a 2017 Treasury Inspector General audit, 1.4 million illegal immigrants who filed tax returns using Individual Taxpayer Identification Numbers (ITINs) also used stolen Social Security numbers on their employer-required W-2 forms. ITINs are available to foreign workers who don't have Social Security numbers, but they are also used by illegal aliens from whom the IRS allegedly wants to collect taxes. The idea that these illegals pay more to the IRS than they get in tax returns is not only unlikely, we know it is untrue. In 2010, of the three million returns filed with ITINs, 2.3 million paid no federal income taxes, and the remainder who did contributed $870 million in federal taxes. But $4.2 billion was paid out to ITIN filers as Additional Child Tax Credits.[46]

Under President Obama, congressional Democrats pushed an amnesty proposal for illegal immigrants that would have granted them access to even more federal tax dollars by allowing them to claim Earned Income Tax Credits for previous years, even if they had never filed a return—something that Koskinen confirmed in writing.[47]

All of this is to say that illegal immigrants do indeed have significant financial incentives to engage in widespread identity theft and to vote for Democrats who steer them benefits.

When authorities discover fraudulent voting, it is often because they are investigating other crimes involving fraudulent identity documents. In 2014, for example, Abel Hernandez-Labra was convicted of passport fraud, identity theft, harboring an illegal alien, *and voting in the 2012 presidential election.*[48] According to Immigration and Customs Enforcement, Hernandez-Labra was a Mexican citizen who entered the United States illegally, purchased the birth certificate and Social Security number of an American citizen, obtained an Iowa driver's license and a U.S. passport, and voted.

The reality is identity theft by illegal immigrants is common nationwide, even in Alaska. Alvaro Jimenez-Aguilar was a Central American who entered the United States in March 2008 on a garden variety six-month travel visa.[49] But as is often the case, he never left. Rather, Jimenez-Aguilar assumed the identity of Andres Kellerman, a U.S. citizen born in Virginia who tragically drowned in 2003 at age twenty-five. Jimenez-Aguilar married Kellerman's aunt. She was also living in the United States illegally.

Court documents describe how Jimenez-Aguilar proceeded to blend into American society and eventually vote. First, he obtained Kellerman's birth certificate, then applied in-person for a duplicate Social Security card in Kellerman's name. Within days, he submitted applications to the Alaska Department of Motor Vehicles using the name, Social Security number, and date of birth belonging to Kellerman.

A year later, in March 2010, he applied to receive a payout from the Alaska Permanent Fund, a state natural resource fund used to subsidize Alaskan residents. One might say he got greedy and was finally caught. It was then discovered that Jimenez-Aguilar was registered to vote.

In February 2017, two Illinois men, Miguel Valencia-Sandoval, thirty-three, and Salvador Garcia-Luna, twenty-seven, were charged with aggravated identity theft—making false claims to U.S. citizenship and "other related crimes."[50] The other related crimes include voting in the 2012, 2014, and 2016 general elections, illegally possessing a firearm, and using stolen identities to obtain U.S. passports.

In another Illinois case, illegal alien Maria Azada was arrested in 2011 and charged with seventeen felony counts relating to voter fraud.[51] Charges against her included perjury, mutilation of election materials, and tampering with voting machines in connection with illegal voting. A criminal investigation revealed Azada allegedly voted nine times between 2003 and 2009. She falsely claimed to be a U.S. citizen on two Illinois voter registration applications. "Our nation's founders reserved the right to vote for U.S. citizens," said Gary Hartwig, an Immigration and Customs Enforcement special agent who worked on the case.

Fredericus Slicher, a citizen of the Netherlands, visited the United States in 1967, and never left.[52] In 1974, Slicher forged a naturalization certificate which he used to obtain a U.S. passport, a Social Security card, and a Maryland driver's license. Had he not appeared as a foreign national in the Maryland Sex Offender Registry in 2013, Slicher might still be on the loose. He voted in federal elections for more than thirty years despite being a noncitizen.

Even foreign drug dealers are in on the action.

Ricardo Lopez-Munguia, forty-five, pleaded guilty[53] to three felony counts of voter fraud in 2012. The California criminal alien admitted to being convicted of two drug trafficking offenses in 1986 involving heroin. A judge ordered him deported as an aggravated felon, but Lopez-Munguia assumed the identity of a U.S. citizen and illegally reentered the United States. According to his guilty plea, Lopez-Munguia obtained a Social Security card and a U.S. passport, and voted.

"Whether we're protecting the integrity of the legal immigration system, rooting out voter fraud, or uncovering identity theft, ICE Homeland Security Investigations is committed to aggressively investigating fraud that undermines our nation's bedrock institutions," said Derek Benner, the special agent in charge for Homeland Security Investigations in San Diego.[54]

While federal immigration and law enforcement officers are indeed committed to protecting our borders and the sanctity of American institutions, much of their effectiveness is determined by who resides in the White House.

The Supreme Court has established that Congress has ultimate authority over immigration policy and the President, as chief executive of the federal bureaucracy, carries out those policies.[55] But as presidential administrations differ, so do their approaches to the enforcement of federal immigration laws.

According to the conservative Heritage Foundation, the Obama administration, for example, constantly sought to "evade, skirt, and ignore" federal immigration laws that were already on the books. A 2010 whitepaper by the group called out the administration for failing to faithfully execute acts of Congress, as is every president's constitutional duty,[56] and charged that the Obama administration had "placed unnecessary new financial and administrative burdens on states and localities (trying to enforce federal immigration laws). The Heritage Foundation also said the Obama administration limited the ability of state and local law enforcement to check the immigration status of those arrested to individuals arrested for 'serious offenses.'"[57]

These policies had their effect. Deportations of illegal immigrants plummeted during the Obama administration. While the Obama administration technically presided over an historic rate of "border deportations," or people being turned away at the border, what are called "interior deportations," or deportations of illegal immigrants who are already residing in the country, fell 73 percent from 2009 to 2016.[58]

President Obama and the Democratic Party favor unrestricted immigration and lax enforcement of voter integrity laws because they assume they gain a large electoral benefit in doing so. Days before the November 2016 election, a young Hispanic interviewer asked Obama, "Many of the millennials, Dreamers, undocumented citizens—and I call them citizens because they contribute to this country—are fearful of voting. So, if I vote, will Immigration know where I live? Will they come for my family and deport us?"[59]

Obama responded: "Not true. And the reason is, first of all, when you vote, you are a citizen yourself. And there is not a situation where the voting rolls somehow are transferred over and people start investigating, et cetera. The sanctity of the vote is strictly confidential." The president's ambiguous answer allowed some to claim that he was only advocating legal voting *on behalf* of illegal immigrants, though other listeners assumed he was encouraging noncitizens to vote because they would likely never get caught. That suspicion was underlined one month prior to the election by Art Del Cueto, vice president for the National Border

Patrol Council, a union representing eighteen thousand Border Patrol agents and support personnel. Del Cueto warned presidential candidate Donald Trump at a New York City roundtable event that Border Patrol agents had been advised not to deport illegal immigrants—even those with criminal records—because the administration wanted "to hurry up and fast track" the immigration status of noncitizens "so they can go ahead and vote in the election."[60]

The National Border Patrol Council said it possessed an internal email from the United States Citizen and Immigration Service showing that "extra overtime is being provided to employees to process as many applications for citizenship as possible prior to November 8." The Council also said it had text messages from upper level managers saying that criminal prosecution cases involving aliens would be put on hold until judges could adjudicate their applications for citizenship.[61] The information tracks with documents obtained by Judicial Watch, showing that the Obama administration spent tens of millions of dollars expediting immigration procedures ahead of the November elections.[62]

Several months earlier, Del Cueto had testified to a congressional subcommittee on border and maritime security that criminality along the border was a serious problem.[63] He said that in 2000, the final year of a different Democratic administration, U.S. authorities arrested 616,000 illegal immigrants in the Tucson, Arizona, sector of the border alone. To put this in perspective, the entire population of Tucson in 2000 was 486,000.

That was one of the worst years for illegal immigration in terms of numbers. But today, he said, the biggest problem is that Mexican drug cartels operate with near-impunity along America's southern border, pushing narcotics and illegal immigrants into the United States.

It's big business.

Not only is America confronting massive illegal immigration along our southern border, but much of it is now being facilitated by Mexican drug cartels who certainly have no compunction against bring criminals across the border.[64]

How likely are such illegal immigrants to get registered to vote? It is hard to say without a thorough analysis of voting rolls. But in 2014, researchers at Old Dominion University in Virginia published a groundbreaking scientific review of noncitizen voting in the 2008 national election.[65] The study relied on data gathered by Harvard University's Cooperative Congressional Election Study, a nationally representative survey of tens of thousands of voters that is taken every two years. The report concluded that:

- Noncitizens cast votes in U.S. elections despite legal bans.
- Noncitizens favor Democratic candidates over Republican candidates.
- Noncitizen voting likely altered Electoral College votes and the composition of Congress.
- Voter photo-identification rules have a limited effect on noncitizen participation.[66]

Authors Jesse Richman, director of the Old Dominion University Social Science Research Center, and David Earnest, associate dean for Research and Graduate Studies at the Old Dominion University College of Arts and Letters, wrote in the *Washington Post* that more than 80 percent of noncitizen votes in their study favored Barack Obama, and that noncitizen voting in Minnesota likely flipped a U.S. Senate election to Democrat Al Franken.[67]

The margin of victory in the Minnesota race was just 312 votes, or 0.65 percent of the state's total noncitizen population. The result of the Minnesota election, they said, likely gave Senate Democrats the pivotal sixtieth vote they needed to overcome filibusters and pass the Affordable Care Act, also known as Obamacare.

Richman and Earnest also said that noncitizen voting may have delivered North Carolina to then-candidate Obama in 2008. Obama won North Carolina by 14,171 votes, or 5.1 percent of the state's adult noncitizen population.

The study's authors said they set out to avoid accusations of playing politics by strictly relying on the Cooperative Congressional Election Study data.[68] Using that data they estimated that 6.4 percent of noncitizens in the United States likely voted in the 2008 presidential election, which equated to 1.2 million votes. But the total number of noncitizen votes, could, they guessed, have been as high as 2.8 million.[69]

The Old Dominion study was immediately attacked, and after being accused of "contributing to a circus," and "providing fuel to conspiracy theorists," authors Richman and Earnest responded to their critics in the *Washington Post*, writing "We trust that our colleagues do not mean to suggest that authors should self-censor findings that speak to contentious debates."[70]

The researchers who conducted the Harvard/YouGov Cooperative Congressional Election Study (CCES) claimed that the Old Dominion analysis was biased and wrong, that its conclusions could be "completely accounted for by very low frequency measurement error," and that "the likely percent of noncitizen voters in recent US elections is 0."[71]

Interestingly, Samantha Luks of YouGov, co-researcher to the CCES data project and coauthor of the Harvard/YouGov denunciation of the Old Dominion study, contributed to the Democratic Congressional Campaign Committee in July 2016, according to the Center for Responsive Politics.[72] Fellow researcher Brian Schaffner also donated to the Hillary Clinton campaign in 2016.[73]

More than one hundred mostly liberal professors also chimed in. They wanted the Old Dominion study effectively banned from the public eye. In an open letter, they declared the study was incorrect and "should not be cited or used in any debate over fraudulent voting."[74] The news media then claimed the study had been "debunked."

The authors of the Old Dominion study, however, stand by their research, even issuing a follow-up report in 2017. Richman and Earnest noted that the Harvard/YouGov critique "falls short for several reasons," including a "lack of statistical power," and "problems with the assumptions" behind their modeling.[75]

A separate study by a research institute called Just Facts, using the same CCES data, found an even larger potential noncitizen voting population. The independent conservative-leaning think tank, estimated that as many as 7.9 million adult noncitizens were registered to vote in 2008, and as many as 5.7 million could have voted.[76]

Speaking to the *Washington Times*, Just Facts president James D. Agresti explained the differing results between the studies. "The details are technical, but the figure I calculated is based on a more conservative margin of sampling error and a methodology that I consider to be more accurate," he said.[77] Agresti noted that the Harvard/YouGov rebuttal of the Old Dominion study assumed that all of the self-reporting noncitizen voters in the CCES data either did not actually vote or mistakenly said they weren't citizens when in fact they were. This, he said, failed to account for both widespread identity theft (with noncitizens having fraudulent documentation that they are citizens) and the fact that noncitizens were far more likely to claim to be citizens than vice versa.[78]

Does this vindicate President Trump's claim of three million illegal voters delivering the popular vote to Hillary Clinton? Not according to the Old Dominion authors. Wary of being drawn into the political fray, author Jesse Richman wrote on an Old Dominion University political science department blog that his 2014 study of the 2008 election should not be applied to the 2016 election.

Moreover, he wrote, it did not provide evidence of voter fraud at the level some Trump administration officials were asserting.[79]

Agresti, however, suspects the number of noncitizens voting in 2016 was potentially much greater than in 2008, because candidate Trump's promise to crack down on illegal immigration likely incentivized many noncitizens to vote against him. In addition, there was a substantially larger pool of noncitizens in the country. President Obama "had publicly stated that election records are not cross-checked against immigration databases" and thus "let noncitizens know that they stand little chance of being caught if they vote," he said. Plus, the Obama administration supported a "court injunction to prevent Kansas, Alabama, and Georgia from requiring people to provide proof of citizenship in order to register to vote," Agresti added.[80]

One has to wonder why the Democratic Party is so keen on opposing electoral integrity laws that ensure only citizens vote. The answer, given the long history of voter fraud, seems pretty obvious.

5

Fraud by Mail—the Problem with Absentee Ballots

Louisville, Kentucky, in the nineteenth century certainly had its share of colorful characters, but John Whallen might be the most memorable. He'd joined the Confederate Army in 1862 at just eleven years old, carrying gunpowder to the batteries as a "powder monkey," and would later relish his status as the "youngest Confederate veteran in the United States."[1]

By the mid-1880s, Whallen and his brother James became the dominant political players in "Whiskey City." He owned the Buckingham Theatre, a burlesque featuring an upstairs "green room" that entertained so many politicians it was known as "the political sewer through which the political filth of Louisville runs."[2]

The city had recently been the first in the United States to adopt the Australian secret ballot. But that kind of reform interfered with Whallen's plans. He was backing a candidate who was facing likely defeat in an upcoming primary election, so "the Buckingham Boss" suggested that Democratic primary voters be told to remain at home one of two nights, and pollsters could come by and ask them which candidate they preferred—essentially, the first form of absentee voting in the country's history.

Whallen sold the idea on the premise it would prevent the crowds at the polls where "liquor, money and bullying can get in their work." And while that may have been true, it also worked to Whallen's profound advantage. Going door-to-door ensured that bought votes were delivered, and unbought votes weren't necessarily counted. Whallen's candidate won.[3]

Today, absentee voting is done by mail, and was intended as a limited way to allow people who wish to vote but cannot get to the polls because of military service, travel, or illness to do so. But it has become an increasingly popular form of voting, and not just for the 1.4 million military members serving overseas. Whether for convenience on Election Day, travel schedules of voters, or for strategic political ends, the numbers of mail-in ballots are on the rise. In 2012, nearly thirty million people cast absentee or mail-in ballots, more than triple the number of people who cast absentee ballots in 1980.[4]

Twenty states require a voter to provide an excuse to receive an absentee ballot; twenty-seven states, plus the District of Columbia, offer absentee ballots on request; and three states conduct all elections by mail. Absentee voting is increasingly popular but also easily exploitable for voter fraud.

Miami-Dade, Florida, State Attorney Katherine Fernandez Rundle noted that "Of the three methods of voting, the one that has always been the most vulnerable, the one where we know fraud has occurred historically...is in the absentee-ballot process....It's the least monitored." The 2005 Commission on Federal Election Reform came to the same conclusion: "Absentee ballots remain the largest source of voter fraud."[5]

As the *New York Times* points out, "On the most basic level, absentee voting replaces the oversight that exists at polling places with something akin to an honor system."[6] And some voters aren't all that honorable.

One Florida newspaper investigating absentee ballot abuses found "credible evidence of fraud" all over the state. And while absentee ballot fraud can come in all shapes and sizes, one population is targeted more than most.

"The problem," a former county attorney in Miami noted, "is really with the collection of absentee ballots at the senior citizen centers," where political campaign staff "help people vote absentee. And help is in quotation marks." They call it "granny farming."[7]

The dependent elderly are easy prey for subtle manipulation or outright fraud. But they aren't the only ones who get victimized. As the *New York Times* points out, "absentee ballots also make it much easier to buy and sell votes."[8]

Missouri State Representative Penny Hubbard was the matriarch of a political dynasty in St. Louis. Her husband Rodney was a fifth ward committeeman. Her son Rodney Jr. is a former State Representative and his twin brother was employed by the city. Penny Hubbard's daughter Tammika is an alderwoman for the city's fifth ward, and her daughter-in-law Shameem is a twenty-sixth ward committeewoman.

The Hubbard family did particularly well among voters who cast absentee ballots. In fact, an analysis by an attorney for a Hubbard 2016 challenger found that in the two previous elections, 95 percent of the absentee ballots in some precincts went to either Representative Penny Hubbard or her daughter Tammika. Indeed, more than 70 percent of absentee ballots were routinely cast for the Hubbards, which far outpaced their popularity at regular polling stations.

As the attorney wrote, "In election after election, an impossibly high percentage of the total number of votes cast in certain precincts—again, particularly in the 5th Ward—were being cast via absentee ballot, and this effect was especially pronounced if a given precinct was involved in an election where a member of the Hubbard family was on the ballot." The attorney's analysis showed "the percentage of absentee ballots being cast tends to plummet whenever a Hubbard is not up for election."[9] Dominating the absentee ballot returns does not necessarily show any fraud. As Hubbard herself has explained, "My entire family has actually been in politics for over five generations. We understand that there are constituents that live in our community. And in the past, they have not come out to vote because some of them have disabilities. They're handicapped. They're sick and too ill to come out. So, when they mentioned to us that they're not going to be able to come to the poll…we engage in the absentee process."[10]

And when the Hubbards engage, they certainly do get results, often from one source in particular.

The *St. Louis Post-Dispatch* reported that on numerous occasions, Hubbard's husband Rodney Sr. "routinely delivered stacks of absentee ballots to the Election Board offices."[11]

Sometimes, according to former election board employees, there would be so many that Hubbard would have to deliver them in postal crates. Despite a state law saying only a second-degree relative can hand-deliver ballots, the city's Election Board accepted them. Many of the ballots were purportedly from voters who lived in the housing units run by Hubbard Sr.'s tenant management company.

Even when election board employees complained about the seeming inappropriateness of Hubbard Sr.'s behavior, their emails went unanswered.

"He brought in a ton of them in a rack, a mail rack," said Patricia Bingham, a former Elections Board employee. "We were telling him we couldn't take it. There were words passed. You don't just tell him you can't do certain things."[12]

Hubbard's power with absentee ballots was such that, even when the election board staff tried to honor the law and refuse the ballots, Hubbard's batch of ballots would "mysteriously appear elsewhere in the office."[13]

The Hubbards were able to get away with this for years because, as the *Post-Dispatch* report noted, St. Louis Election Board employees don't record the names of people who drop off the absentee ballots.

That changed in 2016, when a group of candidates challenging the Hubbards for their respective offices, sounded the alarm before that summer's primary elections. Their lawyer commissioned the study that detailed how much impact the Hubbards and their innovative ballot delivery methods were having on local elections.

Despite this, on the evening of August 2, Representative Penny Hubbard claimed another hard-fought victory over her whistle-blowing opponent. Local activist Bruce Franks captured 53 percent of the votes cast at the polls on Election Day, but Hubbard won the race by a total of ninety votes, winning nearly 80 percent of the absentee ballots.[14] She wasn't the only member of her family to win that way.

Penny's husband Rodney, the ballot-delivery man himself, also eked out a narrow win for reelection to his seat as party committeeman, thanks to capturing more than 70 percent of the absentee ballots, thus winning his election by just fifty-three votes.[15]

Candidates running against the Hubbards cried foul. Their attorney noted that 3 percent of all registered voters in Representative Hubbard's district cast absentee ballots—a total that exceeded "by far the percentage of all voters casting absentee ballots in any other state legislative race on the ballot in St. Louis City."[16]

The Franks campaign sued. The *St. Louis Post-Dispatch* began an investigation and what it discovered provided evidence of voter fraud on behalf of the Hubbards. Reynal Caldwell Jr. told reporters that Hubbard campaign workers knocked on his door a few weeks before the primary election. They asked him to sign something—and he did so, just "to get them off my porch."

A few days after the Hubbard campaign's visit, four other people showed up at Caldwell's door, asking if his absentee ballot had arrived.

"I really don't know who to vote for. The woman I was talking to said she'll put down the same votes as hers."

The Hubbard campaign officials left with Caldwell's signed return envelope and his blank absentee ballot.

Caldwell admitted to the *Post-Dispatch* that he never voted himself. But that's not what the records show. The *Post-Dispatch* investigation found that an absentee ballot was cast by Caldwell in that election. It also found that other residents had a similar experience at the 358-unit Clinton-Peabody housing complex where he lived, and at other neighborhoods in the district.

The Clinton-Peabody housing complex was owned by a development company with business ties to a local real estate mogul named Paul McKee. McKee had donated to many of the Hubbards' various campaigns, and had benefitted personally from their electoral success. As an alderwoman, Tammika Hubbard led the charge to give McKee millions in tax dollars for a development project in the Hubbards' district.[17]

McKee also owns a housing nonprofit that employs Hubbard Sr. as executive director, enabling him to have significant power over tenants in complexes like Clinton-Peabody.

Deirra Paster was one of those tenants who lived in Clinton-Peabody. A few minutes after she spoke with a *Post-Dispatch* reporter about her experiences with the Hubbard campaign and absentee ballots, Paster said she saw a car positioned near her complex, with the female driver taking pictures of the buildings. Paster's friend was able to take pictures of the car's license plate, which was an unusual one. The plate, she said, looked like the kind that is issued to state representatives. It read "R-78." Representative Penny Hubbard represented Missouri's seventy-eighth district.

Thelma Williams spoke to the newspaper. She lived in a different housing complex managed by Rodney Hubbard Sr. Elections Board records showed that three absentee ballots had been requested in her name. When asked about her multiple requests, Williams, eighty-seven, was stumped.

"I didn't fill out but one," she told the reporters. "I mailed mine in. It was mailed to me and I filled it back out."[18]

A judge assessing the evidence nullified the results of the August 2 primary and ordered a new election. This time, the ballots cast on Election Day were decisive. Franks defeated Penny Hubbard, capturing more than 75 percent of the vote, and Rodney Hubbard Sr. lost his race as well.

Without the legal challenge from the Franks campaign and Stephen Deere's and Doug Moore's reporting in the *St. Louis Post-Dispatch*, the Hubbard family would have continued their run of electoral success by stuffing the ballot box with absentee votes.

While the Hubbard saga may be unique to east St. Louis, the lack of oversight by a governing authority, or the complicity of it, is not. Other politicians exploit these electoral vulnerabilities with absentee voting, and the problem only grows.

Incorporated in 1887, Eatonville, Florida, was one of the country's first self-governing all-black municipalities. With a population just over two thousand people, eight churches, and three traffic lights, this small suburb north of Orlando is perhaps best known as home to author Zora Neale Hurston, who featured her hometown in her seminal work *Their Eyes Were Watching God*. The city, in turn, embraces its famous native, naming its library for the author in 2004 and hosting an arts and humanities festival every winter in Hurston's honor.

Unfortunately, the historic town appears to have been celebrating a different tradition at the polls for the past few decades as well.

First elected to city council at age twenty-six, Anthony Grant has been a mainstay of Eatonville local government since 1991. A protégé of former mayor Ada Sims, Grant's tenure was marred from the beginning by allegations of voter fraud. The day after Grant was sworn in as city commissioner, the state's then-Governor Lawton Chiles suspended him from office over allegations of not following voting procedures and asking non-Eatonville residents to fill out absentee ballots.[19]

That Grant would be accused of unscrupulous behavior was no surprise to those who had known the slender, angular-faced, and fast-talking Grant. Two of Grant's former bosses wrote, "He is extremely manipulative of the people around him," in a memo to the Maitland Police officer advisory board when Grant applied for a position. Grant's old supervisors would give him credit for honesty of purpose, if not in deed, noting, "He openly admits to taking advantage of the system by stretching the rules as far as he can."

History has proven how right Grant's former bosses were.

In his first decade as an elected official, Grant was investigated by the Florida Department of Law Enforcement for taking a bribe from a strip club developer, faced a recall petition, and endured a state ethics inquiry over questionable behavior with voter registration envelopes.

Grant's questionable behavior would only benefit his political career.

Grant served as Eatonville's mayor from 1994 to 2009 thanks in large part to his ability to generate absentee ballots. Fellow City Commissioner Alvin Moore said Grant's tactics were well known.

"Mr. Grant would (when helping a voter fill out the absentee ballot request form) put on the return address to one particular person," Moore told me. "So you if you request them all on Monday, they'll be back on Thursday and so we would see (Grant) running in and out of people's houses the day the ballots dropped. He was always watching the mailman."

Grant would serve as Eatonville mayor for fifteen years before losing to local attorney Bruce Mount. But in 2015 Grant embarked on a political comeback, narrowly defeating the incumbent Mayor Mount, thanks, again, to the overwhelming support of absentee voters.

Bill Cowles, Orange County's supervisor of elections, noted the unusual disparity in the absentee numbers, but chalked it up to the fact "that Mr. Grant is a very experienced long-term political candidate in Eatonville. He's always worked the absentees very hard."[20]

When the Mount campaign asked about the possibility of an investigation by the elections supervisor office, Cowles declined. "All the checks and balances are in place," Cowles said. "It's going to take somebody to come forward with some credible, reliable evidence to support their claim."

The Mount campaign filed a lawsuit against the Orange County Canvassing Board and the Eatonville Canvassing Board, which Grant's lawyers managed to get dismissed on a technicality. But Mount's challenge drew the attention of the Florida Department of Law Enforcement, who determined that some of Grant's absentee voters were truly absentee—they did not live in the town.[21] Grant, who had a sideline managing housing units, was also accused of offering discounted rent to his tenants in exchange for their votes.[22] A single mother who testified against Grant said she feared she would lose her government-subsidized home if she didn't vote for Grant.

"It's hard to get somebody who's not interested in voting to actually drive to the polls to vote on Election Day," prosecutor Richard Walsh explained. "It's not too hard when you bring the ballot to them and stand by them to have you vote in front of them and tell them how to vote."[23]

Although he faced eleven years in prison, Grant got off easy. Despite his conviction on felony voting fraud and felony election violations, Grant was sentenced to just four hundred hours of community service, four years of probation, and the time he had already served in jail. He was also stripped of his mayoral office.

As egregious as Grant's fraudulent vote-getting efforts were, he almost got away with them. He had, in fact, been sworn in as the new mayor, and neither the city of Eatonville nor Orange County's supervisor of elections, the two local authorities responsible for the fairness of the election, had intervened. Ironically, it was only because of the press attention that Grant seemed to crave that the Florida Department of Law Enforcement noticed the claims brought by Mount's lawsuit and decided to investigate. Often the problem is that law enforcement officials are reluctant to follow up even on the most glaring cases of voter fraud.

A *Palm Beach Post* investigation into the 2016 primary elections for county commissioner and multiple state legislature seats uncovered significant evidence of voter fraud through the use of absentee ballots. The paper's comprehensive findings drew a distinction between some of the fraud claims made by Donald Trump, who insisted that "millions of votes" might have been fraudulent across the nation, and the *potential* for that scenario to become reality. "None of *The Post*'s findings support President Donald Trump's claim of millions of illegal votes, but instead suggest a growing facet of the elections system is ill-equipped to prevent voting fraud where it is most susceptible—from inside voters' homes."[24]

Sadly, part of the story of voter fraud isn't just the ballots cast illegally, but the practices that our flawed system actually permits.

What the *Post* found were three candidates, all sharing a common political lineage, employing tactics that, while potentially legal, conflict with the spirit of numerous election laws, according to experts. County Commissioner Mack Bernard, State Representative Al Jacquet, and a candidate for state Senate, Bobby Powell, all ordered ballots on behalf of their constituents, in many cases without those constituents' knowledge. Then, they either filled out the ballot for them or forced them to fill out the ballots while the candidates were present in their home.

Joseph Clerfius, a blind Haitian man, and his wife Antoinette, told the newspaper that County Commissioner Bernard showed up at their door, produced a ballot, filled it out on Clerfius's behalf, and then actually signed Clerfius's name.

"I couldn't sign because I can't see," Clerfius said. "I gave him my voting card number. That's all I did. He wrote my name."[25]

Incredibly, Florida law may not explicitly prohibit candidates from "helping" voters fill out absentee ballots. So Bernard may not have violated the law. But what is *supposed to happen* is that if a voter's signature on an absentee ballot does not match the signature on file with the elections board, that ballot gets flagged. But that didn't happen in Clerfius's case. And as the results would show, in this election, his case would seem to be an example that proved the rule.

The Palm Beach County Elections Supervisor Susan Bucher lamented her office's inability to offer more protections than the law allows.

Bucher told Bernard's opponent, incumbent County Commissioner Priscilla Taylor, that her office received hundreds of absentee ballot request forms, *all* filled out in the same ink and with the same handwriting, *all* delivered by the Bernard campaign. Bucher's office sent letters to three hundred of the voters associated with those requests because the signatures on the request forms didn't match the signatures on file. But the key fact here is that Bucher sent letters to those three hundred only because there was actually a signature on the request form. Florida law doesn't actually require that the prospective absentee voters sign the request form, unless they are also requesting it be mailed to a different address.

Only nineteen of the three hundred people Bucher contacted followed up and confirmed that they had in fact requested an absentee ballot. But Bucher's office sent absentee ballots to all three hundred anyway because Florida law doesn't permit her to discard the requests. Bernard defeated Taylor in the election, despite losing the in-person vote by 768, because of an absentee ballot margin of 1,286.[26]

Jacquet, who worked previously as an aide to Bernard when he was in the Florida Legislature, also enjoyed similar dominance among absentee voters. Jacquet lost his in-person vote by 132, but cruised to a win with 1,167 more mail-in votes than his opponent. Jacquet and Bernard actually combined to collect mail-in ballots at levels highly unusual for local elections. In the August primary in which Bernard and Jacquet ran, candidates on average received roughly one third of their votes via absentee. But Jacquet and Bernard received *more than half* of their respective votes from absentee voters. In several precincts, Jacquet and Bernard received more votes than candidates running for the U.S. Senate, a highly unusual outcome. In one precinct, Bernard and Jacquet received nine out of every ten absentee ballots cast.

Calling the results "highly suspect," Daniel Smith, a University of Florida political science professor whose focus is elections, noted that "When you have isolated precincts where a certain candidate overperformed, it raises questions about what those voters were thinking in marking their ballots. Or whether those voters marked their ballots at all."[27]

The safeguards meant to prevent exactly this type of fraud failed to do so, the *Post* investigation showed. And when legal authorities were presented after the election with the evidence, they did nothing. Bucher, the supervisor of elections, raised concern about "certain political campaigns" committing voter fraud months before the August 30, 2016, primary. She asked the state attorney's public corruption unit to investigate *two months* before the election.

After the election, Michael Steinger, the lawyer who lost to Bobby Powell in his state Senate race, hired a private investigator who provided affidavits from twenty-two voters, alleging fraud. Despite the advance warnings from Bucher, the unusual results and complaints by the losing campaigns, detectives working for the Palm Beach state attorney waited eight months to interview some of the witnesses and voters who complained about absentee ballot request forms having been submitted in their names. It wasn't until the *Palm Beach Post* ran a series of stories in April 2017 that the detectives finally interviewed some of the key witnesses, including forty voters and the elections supervisor. But they did not interview any voters in the precincts where the newspaper found the strongest evidence for fraud, including the precinct where Bernard and Jacquet won 90 percent of all absentee ballots cast.

Ultimately, despite finding video of a Powell aide dropping off "bundles" of ballot request forms, unusual financial cooperation between all three campaigns, and a political consulting firm owned by an aide to Bernard, detectives claimed they couldn't find a suspect.

State Attorney Dave Aronberg, a Democrat and former State Representative, decided not to press charges.[28] And Senator Powell threatened the *Palm Beach Post* for its reporting. "It's distasteful," Powell told an audience at a public forum shortly after the paper's reporting was published. "It should be criminal that newspapers can print something like that and implicate."[29] Jacquet, who attended the forum with Powell, took aim at the Sheriff's deputies who conducted interviews with voters. He called the deputies' conduct "criminal" and "unconstitutional."

"Someone comes to your door in uniform, bangs on your door and says, 'Who did you vote for? How did you vote for them? Why did you vote for them? Did they give you anything to vote for them?'" Jacquet charged. "This is not only criminal, this is unconstitutional civil rights violations. This is singling out one group of folks and literally intimidating them, suppressing their right to vote."

Many of the voters in the Palm Beach case were, like Jacquet himself, of Haitian descent. When contacted by the *Post* about the irregularities in absentee ballot patterns, Jacquet struck a familiar tone.

"I worked hard and played by the rules! No laws were broken. I will not answer to your trumped-up scare tactics. Blacks have been terrorized long enough!" the first-term state House member wrote. "Please reassure me that this is not discrimination and a distraction in [an] effort to destroy black progress and increase a dying circulation. Working twice as hard for half the respect is all too familiar."[30]

It is possible to both understand the obstacles overcome by racial minorities in securing equal voting rights and to also highlight the gaping vulnerabilities in our current election rules for absentee balloting. The Palm Beach County state attorney's investigation found that "typically, voters who are solicited are located in 'low income' areas."[31] These areas of concentrated poverty or foreign immigrants include people who have little political awareness or motivation to vote, or do not possess much knowledge about the laws concerning voting. Such areas around the country become fertile ground for political operatives hoping to exploit vulnerable people for their own political and professional gain. Absentee ballot fraud is so common in Florida, in fact, there's even a specialized name for people who make their living hustling absentee ballots: the *boleteros*.

Boleteros (Spanish for 'balloteer') are essentially absentee-ballot brokers, paid to collect and turn out absentee ballots throughout the state, especially in the Hispanic enclaves of South Florida.

Democratic political consultant Christian Ulvert is one of Florida's top political operatives, managing campaigns all over the state. He says, "These boleteros in Miami-Dade have become like some political consultants. You don't want them working for you. But you don't want them working *against* you. So, some candidates figure you just have to pay them."

Ulvert acknowledges these *boleteros* operate on the "edge of the spirit of the law." But many seem to cross the line. The case of one famous South Florida *boletera* shows just how these political operatives and candidates operate in the shadows.

Fifty-six-year-old Miami resident Deisy Cabrera was charged in 2013 with a felony for forging the signature of an elderly woman and being in possession of more than two absentee ballots. Cabrera was found to have illegally collected at least thirty-one ballots before one primary election, though the ballots she illegally possessed may have been the least interesting part of her case. Cabrera was also found with notebooks detailing her network of more than five hundred voters in the Miami area, many of them senior citizens. Her ledger also listed multiple candidates for elected judgeships, along with notations of payments from the candidates.

It is not illegal to pay political consultants, and three of the candidates in Cabrera's notebooks had filed paperwork declaring a total of $1,650 in payments to Cabrera.[32] But Cabrera's notebooks indicated she had collected more than $10,000 from seven candidates.

Ultimately, Cabrera pleaded guilty to two misdemeanor counts of violating a county ordinance against possessing more than two ballots that belong to another voter. The felony charge against Cabrera for forging the signature of an elderly woman in a nursing home was dropped, because the woman died before Cabrera could be prosecuted. But a local newspaper interviewed more than two dozen other nursing home residents who said Cabrera regularly came to them and "helped" with their absentee ballots. Many of the voters, when asked by reporters whom they had voted for, had no idea. Cabrera was sentenced to a year's probation.

The problem is hardly limited to South Florida. In 2013, more public officials were convicted of corruption in the Rio Grande Valley of South Texas than in any other part of the country. And while those politicians were caught by FBI and DOJ investigations, a related cottage industry of corruption remains open for business.

If South Florida has their *boleteros*, South Texas has *politiqueros*—locals who collect good money delivering questionable votes. Like their Florida counterparts, *politiqueros* prefer one particular technique. As an NPR story on the *politiqueros* noted, "Hustling votes has a rich political history in America. Chicagoans have been known to vote from beyond the grave. Democratic machines from New Orleans to New York City have hauled voters to the polls. In the Valley, it's all about mail-in ballots."

Herminia Becerra, one of the only participants who would speak on record, boasted to NPR about her ability to round up any number of votes for political candidates. Becerra, one of many hundreds of paid campaign workers who operate in the region, attributes her success to simply informing voters about her candidate.[33]

"Oh, yes. I know it can be done because I've done it," she says without hesitation. "I know lots of people, and people know me. If I do a favor for you, you're grateful and your whole family is grateful. And you're going to tell your whole family, 'Help Herminia.'"

Ardent supporters of the *politiqueros* system say they are really just campaign staffers, and insist that these helpers are crucial to elections, given South Texas's historically poor voter turnout numbers.[34] Low turnout in Texas is a reasonable concern, given that only 33 percent of registered voters participated in the state's 2014 gubernatorial election, and turnout in McAllen and Brownsville is less than half the registered population.[35]

Though the entire *politiqueros* system is legal, it is under heavy criticism from candidates for public office who decry the corrupt election scheme. Legally, paid workers are allowed to canvass, help voters fill out absentee ballots if they are unable, and deliver the votes.

But often, the *politiqueros* take it one step further.

In Donna, Texas, five *politiqueros* admitted to bribing voters with beer, cigarettes, and dime bags of cocaine.

Assistant U.S. Attorney James Sturgis lamented that "the *politiqueros* are being paid to then go and essentially round up voters and have them vote a certain way."

As in other parts of the country, vulnerable populations like the elderly are an easy target for would-be fraudsters in South Texas. Mary Helen Flores, the founder of Citizens Against Voter Abuse, said she's spoken with hundreds of elderly residents, and says the *politiqueros* target them.

"[The voter] has been cultivated by this particular *politiquera* who works that building to give up her vote every election," Flores says. "And the [*politiquera*] will, under the guise of helping her, come and take her ballot from her and say: 'Well, I'm going to go mail it for you.'"

While *politiqueros* are used in state and federal elections, they are far more useful and common in county elections, where just a few hundred votes can tip the scales in one candidate's favor, and where corrupt bureaucrats might give the system a wink and a nod.[36] Representative José Luis Aliseda testified before federal court in *Texas v. Eric Holder* about the nature of *politiqueros* in Bee County.[37] Essentially, they would encourage elderly people to sign up for a mail-in ballot, and then shadow the postmen delivering the ballots to the voters' homes. They would helpfully guide the voter's choice. Aliseda noted an investigation into a district attorney's race that was decided by nineteen votes, with eighteen votes being coming from individuals whose listed age was more than 110 years old.[38]

Despite the controversy, it's not a bad gig to be a *politiquero*; they get paid anywhere between $5 and $25 per vote delivered and a chance for a job provided by the elected official.[39] Some *politiqueros* even moved to the big leagues, harvesting votes for Hillary Clinton when she campaigned in South Texas in 2008. One reporter revealed that the Clinton campaign paid 460 *politiqueros* during her Texas campaign.[40]

The good news, in South Texas at least, is that the attention of federal law enforcement seems to be working. From 2012 to 2014, with ongoing federal probes and indictments, the number of mail-in ballots dropped 97 percent.[41]

Boleteros, *politiqueros*, and practitioners of absentee ballot fraud often evade prosecution because of ambiguities in the law. Campaign workers are allowed to request absentee ballots for voters. Many local ordinances even allow them to "assist" voters who need help because of physical incapacity, inability to read English, or even mental conditions. Absentee ballots must be requested using a signed request form. Elections officials record how many requests they receive and the absentee ballots they send out during each election cycle. But an analysis performed by the Center for Public Integrity found that more one in eight precincts they studied had received, rejected, or counted more ballots than they sent.[42]

Elections officials dismiss such findings as mere evidence of administrative snafus, not widespread voter fraud. But with no attempt at verifying that votes cast by absentee ballots come from actual voters voting of their own free will, true accountability for the integrity of absentee ballots is impossible. And it affects races all over the country.

Three states—Colorado, Oregon, and Washington—conduct all elections by mail, sending ballots by post to all eligible voters in each election. In nineteen other states, certain elections may be held by mail. Eight states and the District of Columbia also maintain a "permanent absentee ballot" list, meaning these voters will automatically receive an absentee ballot for all future elections without having to request it.

This is bad news to advocates of better election security. More ballots completed outside polling places may be convenient for voters, but it also makes them far more susceptible to malfeasance and mischief by the bad actors of the political world. As long as the laws permit political insiders like the Hubbards in St. Louis, the *boleteros* of South Florida, or the *politiqueros* of Texas to request ballots for voters and deliver those ballots both to the voter and the polling place, absentee votes today aren't really much safer than the ones supposedly cast in 1892 in Louisville, helpfully gathered by John Whallen's cronies going door-to-door. Voter fraud, unfortunately, is not merely part of country's colorful past, but a very corrupt part of our political present.

CHAPTER

6

Who's Running This Thing Anyways?—the Counters

Hearings of Florida's Clemency Board always make for interesting theater. Comprised of Florida's governor, attorney general, the chief financial officer of the state's Department of Financial Services, and the agriculture commissioner, the board hears appeals from convicted felons seeking to have their civil rights restored.

Learlean Rahming, of Miami, approached the podium in September 2016. Officials were impressed that, after facing numerous charges, including larceny, drug possession, and shoplifting, she had been able to turn her life around and stay out of trouble—and prison—for the past two decades. CFO Jeff Atwater asked, "What happened that you were able to turn this around?"

"Ah, gosh," Rahming replied. "I completed drug treatment, because I had a drug problem, and, I just wanted to do the right thing, and that's what I've been doing for years. I just turned my life around. I got tired."

Florida's Governor Rick Scott was impressed. "I move to grant restoration of rights," he said.

But there was one problem.

Attorney General Pam Bondi interjected, "Can I just ask a question, governor? It says here that you told the parole commissioners that you voted countless times when you were a felon. But then, you said you didn't realize you couldn't vote."

"Right," Rahming replied.

"But then, it says you received a letter saying that your name was removed from the voter roll," Bondi continued. "And then you registered under a different name and continued to vote? After you received the letter?"

Rahming explained that she didn't realize that, as a convicted felon, she wasn't able to vote.

"I wasn't aware that I didn't have my rights back, 'cause I used to work for the election department," she told the board.

Governor Scott pressed Rahming on the specifics. "Here's what this says. You registered to vote under the name Lolean A. Roahming in Miami-Dade County and on September 9, 2000, um....So you voted a bunch of times, then so, then you were removed, so then you reregistered under the name Lerlean Arthur Roahming-Wayne."

"That's my marriage name," Rahming replied.

"So why would you, why would you, if you've been told you couldn't register, why did you register?" Scott asked incredulously.

Rahming's response would prove damning: "Just to see if I could vote."

Scott denied her appeal for restoration of rights, and Rahming, along with her daughter who had flown to Tallahassee from Texas to support her mother's effort, left the courthouse in tears.

It may seem surprising that Rahming didn't know, as an employee of an elections office, what the rules were. But when it comes to voter rolls and election officials, you should never take anything for granted. In fact, sometimes it appears that state officials are inclined to break the rules.

In July 2008, Montana's Democratic Governor Brian Schweitzer nearly confessed to doing just that.

Addressing a convention of trial lawyers in Philadelphia—a reliably Democratic crowd—Schweitzer reminisced about how he helped elect a Democrat as a United States senator in a largely Republican state. "When you have the Governor of a state on your side," he said, "you can turn some dials. And we did. For example…seven percent of the population are Indian…and when they vote, they vote for Democrats. So we wanted to make sure they voted. We did all of our homework. We made sure they were all registered. We made sure they went to a poll on election day. And we anticipated some of the shenanigans from those fools back east."[1]

He continued:

> I called the tribal chairs two weeks in advance. [I warned them that] There's likely to be some sons of bitches. They're likely to show up in front of the polling place and they're going to ask them if they have proof that they paid their electric bill, they're gonna tell you that you can't go in and vote if you have any sort of a warrant out for you, if you're not exactly sure if you've got your driver's license and so we didn't want any of that bullshit to go on.

Schweitzer noted the poll watchers were easy to spot because they'd be wearing a "brand new Carhartt jacket, new boots, no cow shit on them. They'll be the only white guys for 50 miles around," and that the tribal chiefs threatened to arrest them if they didn't leave the reservation. Schweitzer was so certain that his candidate, Jon Tester, would win that he called the AP bureau and election officials in Butte on election night to find out why they hadn't yet declared him the winner.

Montana Republicans were outraged at his remarks. They filed complaints with the secretary of state's office and the attorney general, alleging Schweitzer's speech amounted to a confession of voter fraud. Schweitzer insisted he was merely joking.

The clerk and recorder in Butte confirmed Schweitzer's phone call on election night, but said she had refused to speak with him; the AP Bureau chief confirmed that Schweitzer pressured him to call the race before they were ready.

Terry Coddens was a poll worker at predominantly American Indian precincts on election day. He signed an affidavit detailing violations of state law by election workers. Coddens said an elections judge made him leave before officials counted the votes, and that election workers never secured the ballot boxes with locks.[2]

Montana's secretary of state asked the state's attorney general, Mike McGrath, to investigate. But McGrath, a Democrat, declined, saying there was "no allegation supported by fact," to justify an investigation, only the words of "a speaker trying to be funny."[3]

New Hampshire's Secretary of State Bill Gardner, on the other hand, learned that apparent voter fraud is no laughing matter.

Gardner, a Democrat, was horrified at the number of out-of-state residents voting in New Hampshire elections. They could do so, because under state law voters need only have an "intent to reside" in the Granite State.

"We have all kinds of different durational requirements for residency," he said. "You have to be here five years. You have to be here six months, depending on whether it's a fishing license, welfare. The governor has to live here seven years. When Eisenhower came here in the 1950s, he couldn't fish. They had to go to Maine."[4]

But if people are going to Maine to fish because it's easier, they are coming back south to cast a ballot. "We have drive-by voters," Gardner told the *New Hampshire Union Leader.*

In 2008 Gardner saw this firsthand at a polling station when three Americorps volunteers, who were not New Hampshire residents, tried to vote.

"The people that ran the polling place called me over, and said they had three people who didn't know whether they could vote, and they wanted me to answer the questions," he told the *Union Leader.* "So I go over…. I said, 'Where is your home?' The woman said, 'Washington State.' I said, 'Why didn't you vote in Washington State?' She said she missed the deadline, but she really wanted to vote. She said she was going back to Washington State the first of December. I said, 'well that should answer it for yourself as to whether this is now your home.'

"But then one of the guys said, 'Wait, you don't know for sure, you might fall in love with a guy tonight. You don't know for sure.' The woman registered, but wound up not voting. The two men did."

So the top election official in the entire state knows voter fraud exists, because he's seen it. Yet he was, and is, powerless to do anything about it. Every legislative session, he says he hopes the law will get changed.

But even if New Hampshire's law does get changed, it will be too late for Kelly Ayotte.

In 2016 Ayotte lost her bid for reelection to the Senate to Democrat Maggie Hassan by 1,017 votes. This margin became all-the-more notable when it was revealed that 6,500 people voted that cycle with out-of-state driver's licenses. The follow-up reporting also revealed that in the ten months since Ayotte's defeat, only 1,014 of those voters had actually been issued New Hampshire driver's licenses, and only two hundred people had registered a vehicle in the state. What became of the other 5,500 "transplants?"

But New Hampshire's voting laws are strict compared to Minnesota's. In Minnesota you can register to vote on Election Day, and the way you "prove" your residential status has many onlookers crying foul.

Voters who want to register and vote on election day do not need ID or proof of residence, *as long as another voter signs an oath confirming that person's address.* This process is known as "vouching," which has been Minnesota law since 1973.[5] Until 2010, residents with a valid ID were permitted to vouch for up to fifteen voters on election day, until it was reduced to only eight. If this sounds like a recipe for fraudulent exploitation, it is.

In Chapter Two we discussed the story of the George Soros–backed action group called America Coming Together (ACT), which spent more than $10 million on election day in 2004 for 45,000 paid canvassers, along with another 25,000 volunteers, to get out the vote for Democratic presidential candidate John Kerry.

In short, Soros's ACT was making a *coordinated political effort* to take advantage of a lax voting law. ACT ended up paying $775,000 in fines for violating campaign finance laws, and disbanded in 2005, but other groups, some of them Soros-backed, have emerged with similar aims.

In 2010, for instance, members of the Obama-backed group Organizing for America (OFA) were accused of organizing voter fraud.

At the University Lutheran Church in downtown Minneapolis, an election judge saw a woman assigning vouchers confirming Minnesota residency to would-be voters. He asked if she knew the people in her group. The woman said no, but that OFA leaders had told her to do this. Vouching for voters without actual knowledge of their residency status is a felony in Minnesota.

Mike Griffin, the Organizing for America field director, was himself escorted out of the polling precinct when he tried to vouch for a voter who, in the eyes of the elections judge, Griffin did not know.

Of the eight hundred votes cast at the University Lutheran church that day, five hundred of them were on-site registrations. And while the vigilant elections judge had blocked two attempts to subvert election rules, there were no arrests.

While Minnesotans have limits on how many voters they can vouch for (as many as eight on election day), there are exceptions. Workers at residential facilities—including nursing homes, homeless shelters, assisted living facilities, transitional housing, or group homes—are allowed to vouch for every resident. As voter fraud is often perpetrated using the poor or the dependent elderly, this is a significant exception, and in a state like Minnesota, which has had many close elections, could be decisive. In 2008, for example, Al Franken won election to the Senate by 312 votes, less than the documented number of votes cast by convicted felons.

Nearby Wisconsin also has problems with voter fraud, especially in Milwaukee, where police discovered that four thousand more votes were cast than there were registered voters in the 2004 presidential election.

"The Milwaukee homeless vote has the potential to affect the outcome of a local election," the police report said. "This vote portability and the abject poverty that defines homelessness make these unfortunate individuals vulnerable to become the tools of voter fraud."[6]

The Milwaukee Police Department cited same-day registration and voting as a vulnerability to the integrity of the state's elections.

"If a verification period would be provided to the Election Commission before any Election," the report said, "the majority of the problems detailed in this report would not have existed." The report also recommended a requirement that voters produce government-issued ID when going to vote.

But not everyone agreed with those suggestions.

"I don't like either of those ideas and I'm not sure why the Milwaukee Police Department should be the one deciding what the voting policy is of the state of Wisconsin," Democratic Governor Jim Doyle said. Doyle's position is consistent with that of most elected Democrats, who see the lack of ID laws as benefiting their party. And party affiliation is important in this regard because the electoral laws of most states are enforced by elected secretaries of state.

In 2005, a national Commission on Federal Election Reform, co-chaired by former President Jimmy Carter and former Secretary of State James A. Baker III, recommended that elections be supervised by nonpartisan election officers rather than by partisan secretaries of state.

"Partisan officials should not be in charge of elections," said Robert Pastor, the executive director of the Commission. "Both Democrats and Republicans not only compete for power, they try to manipulate the rules to get an advantage. We want to make sure that those counting votes don't have a dog in that game."

Each state has a chief elections officer who, in most cases, is the secretary of state. Some of them are appointed, but most are elected. The role of chief elections officer has greatly expanded in recent years due to sweeping reforms in the National Voter Registration Act of 1993 and the Help America Vote Act of 2002.[7]

The emphasis secretaries of state put on electoral security varies widely. In Kansas, Republican Kris Kobach, elected in 2010, has worked to scrub ineligible voters from the voting rolls. North Carolina's longtime secretary of state, on the other hand, Democrat Elaine Marshall, has allowed certain noncitizens—those covered by the Obama administration's Deferred Action for Childhood Arrivals—to become notary publics who can certify absentee ballots.

State Representative Chris Millis of North Carolina investigated that action, and warned that "the Secretary has commissioned more than 325 alien notaries who can... validate fraudulent votes state-wide, if they are so inclined." Millis added that one "notary commissioned by the Secretary was an alien against whom a final order for deportation existed."[8]

State officials oversee and certify elections done at the state level, but votes, of course, are cast at local precincts, which are overseen by local supervisors of elections. Those officials are ultimately responsible, along with their staff, for keeping accurate, current voter rolls. It's a task that gets neglected quite often.

In 2010, Florida's Republican-controlled legislature ordered state officials to scrub ineligible voters from the rolls before the 2012 presidential election.

State officials discovered that more than 53,000 dead people were still listed as eligible voters, and asked that local elections supervisors check to make sure that noncitizens weren't also registered to vote. The state had identified 2,600 such people on the rolls, but believed that the total number of noncitizens registered to vote in Florida might run as high as 182,000 people.

Many local officials, however, balked at the request.

Pasco County's elections supervisor Brian Corley articulated the political and electoral calculus. "We want our voter rolls to be accurate, obviously no one wants someone to vote who isn't a citizen," Corley said. "But at the same time we are the ones fielding phone calls from voters saying 'Why are you questioning my citizenship?'"[9]

Local officials also expressed their doubts about whether ineligible voters were really a significant problem. The St. Lucie County elections supervisor Gertrude Walker went a step further. "We don't have confidence in the validity of the information."

Imagine that.

Despite federal laws that mandate the maintenance of accurate voter rolls, the reality is that voting rolls all across the country are rife with errors, whether through honest human error or a lack of meaningful oversight and correction. In California, for example, eleven counties have more registered voters than legal residents of voting age; and California is hardly alone.

In October 2016, a local Chicago television station compared the Social Security administration's "death file" with voter records. It found that dead people didn't just stop voting after the election of JFK. The station documented how 119 dead people voted a total of 229 times over the previous ten years. A similar investigation in Los Angeles by KCBS found that 265 dead voters cast ballots "year after year."

An analysis by the Public Interest Legal Foundation showed 248 counties across the country have "more registered voters than live adults."[10] Kentucky had forty-one such counties, the most in the nation, which is interesting considering the very public opposition its Secretary of State Alison Grimes has for releasing voter information. When the Presidential Advisory on Election Integrity asked all states for their voter information, Grimes refused, saying "There's not enough bourbon here in Kentucky to make this request seem sensible....Not on my watch are we going to be turning over something that's left to the states to run...."[11]

Even when state officials do try to remove ineligible or inactive names from the voter rolls, they often run into legal hurdles thrown up by Democratic administrations.

In 2011, Florida Governor Rick Scott, along with officials in Colorado, Michigan, and North Carolina, requested access to the Department of Homeland Security's Systematic Alien Verification for Entitlements (SAVE) national citizenship database. Accessing this information would allow the states to cross-reference people on the voter rolls with the most accurate list of who is eligible to vote.

Florida had already compared its voter rolls against its driver's license applications, and identified 182,000 residents who were noncitizens at the time of their registration. Cross-checking that list with the SAVE database would have shown how many of those people had since become naturalized and were thus eligible to vote.

But the Obama administration didn't think it was such a good idea.

Rather than granting Florida and other states access to that information, Obama's Attorney General Eric Holder sued Florida to prevent Florida from removing anyone from its rolls. Instead of supporting Florida's efforts to comply with federal laws on electoral integrity, Holder accused Florida of violating the 1965 civil rights act.

Chris Cate, spokesman for the Florida Department of State, noted that the state has "a year-round obligation to assure that the voter rolls are accurate. It's not only the right thing to do, it's our statutory responsibility. And at no point in the process of us identifying non-citizens do we look at race or party. The only criterion that concerns us is whether someone is an ineligible voter. If so, that person needs to be removed from the voter rolls. We don't want an ineligible voter to neutralize the vote of an eligible U.S. citizen."[12]

Other officials go the other way, such as Virginia's Democratic Governor Terry McAuliffe. In 2016, he vetoed a measure that would have required investigating any election in which ballots in one precinct exceeded the total number of voters registered in that precinct. He also made formerly ineligible voters eligible. In Virginia, felons are automatically banned from voting unless granted an individual exemption. In April 2017, McAuliffe said his "proudest achievement" as governor was restoring the voting rights of 156,221 convicted felons, which included, Republican critics pointed out and the *Washington Post* noted, "132 sex offenders in custody and...several convicted killers on probation in other states."[13]

McAuliffe justified the restoration of voting rights to felons as a matter of civil rights. But his veto of mandatory investigations when the number of ballots exceeds the number of registered voters would appear to undermine his concern for electoral fraud.

Kansas Secretary of State Kris Kobach, co-chairman of President Trump's now-disbanded Advisory Commission on Election Integrity, makes an obvious point: "When you have an extremely large number of stale names on the voter rolls in a county, it makes voter fraud much easier to commit. It's easier to identify a large number of names of people who have moved away or are deceased. At that point, if there is no photo-ID requirement in the state, those identities can be used to vote fraudulently."[14]

In December 2013, New York City's Department of Investigation issued a report on the New York City Board of Elections. That investigation into possible "fraud, corruption, waste, mismanagement, and conflicts of interest" revealed that "there are names of ineligible voters (*e.g.*, felons and people no longer City residents), and deceased voters, on the [Board of Election] voter rolls, some for periods of up to four years."[15]

New York Department of Investigation officials sent undercover agents to cast ballots on behalf of elderly citizen, felons, and people who had moved. Its officers "were permitted to obtain, mark, and submit ballots in the scanners or in the lever voting booths in 61 [of 63] cases, with no challenge or question by [Board of Election] poll workers."

One of the few unsuccessful attempts occurred when an officer attempted to vote using the name of a felon listed on the rolls, only to be informed by the poll inspector that he was requesting the ballot of the poll worker's son.

When officials didn't have such familial knowledge, no questions were asked, despite glaring red flags. A twenty-six-year-old investigator, for example, was able to cast a ballot on behalf of a former resident who was seventy-six years old. Other investigators told the poll workers that they used to live in New York City and wanted to vote in the election. They were told that if their names were still on the rolls, they could "play dumb" and vote.[16]

Juan Morel Campos Secondary School, otherwise known as IS-71, is the site of one of the busiest polling places in Brooklyn, serving more than 3,200 voters. It's also the primary polling place for rival factions of the Satmar strain of Hasidic Judaism, the Zalis and the Ahronim.[17]

Reporter Jacob Kornbluh told the *Times of Israel*: "They're fighting for leadership. The two factions always support opposing Democratic candidates. By gaining a majority in a pivotal district, the faction can improve its dealing power with future politicians.... Whoever gets the more votes, they will be the kingmaker. They will have all the power," said Kornbluh.

According to Kornbluh, the factions "keep a meticulous registration of their own base, and can supply candidates with the exact number of their votes, be they legitimate or not."

As it turns out, there are plenty of illegitimate votes to be counted.

During the Democratic primary elections in September 2013, numerous on-site observers witnessed a coordinated effort to overwhelm poll workers and cast fraudulent votes.

"They're fourteen, fifteen years old, walking in here with a crowd of people. We stopped them and asked for ID—we know they're too young to go in there. They've been trying it all day," Board of Elections Officer Antoinette Reaves said. "The same faces are appearing."

As the *New York Times* reported, "One 15-year-old voter told Kornbluh he knew of 35 other boys his age voting. The teenager, who voted for Bill Thompson, said he himself had no political inclination, but that 'we are doing this for the rabbi, to win.'"[18]

A source cited by the news site Gothamist.com told the reporters that the fraud was orchestrated. "Volunteers are allegedly given free food and then 'driven to four or five places' to vote under false names. 'They have copies of the voter rolls, I don't know how they get them, but they get the names and the signatures,' the source alleged."[19]

So who is in charge?

The New York Police Department sent additional officers to the polling site on election day to control the crowd, but admitted that voter fraud wasn't under its purview. Ultimately, it's up to elections officials to refer any documented examples or suspicions of fraud to law enforcement authorities. And some election officials are more conscientious than others.

In November 2003, then-Governor Jeb Bush of Florida appointed Dr. Brenda Snipes to the position of Broward County Elections Supervisor.[20] She replaced Miriam Oliphant, whom Bush removed for "repeated and continuing failures… to properly manage her office and take the most basic preparatory steps for the conduct of elections."[21] These included leaving uncounted votes in a cabinet drawer and running the department a million dollars over budget.

Things did not immediately improve under Dr. Snipes. In 2004, nearly 60,000 absentee ballots failed to arrive in the mailboxes of voters, and nearly 20,000 had to be re-sent.[22]

In fact, eight years later it appeared that things had not improved at all. After the 2012 general election, almost a thousand uncounted military ballots were discovered in a warehouse. They were eventually counted, but the incident raised concerns. Snipes defended her office, writing in an open letter to voters that the ballots were "not considered 'lost' and therefore not considered 'found.'"[23]

More problems surfaced a week later.

The *Sun-Sentinel* reported that in 2012, Snipes' office sent absentee ballots to five felons who voted illegally.[24]

Then a 2014 report revealed that Broward County had assigned more than two thousand voters to a phantom voting district, which was allegedly set aside for registered voters whose mail was returned or who were living overseas, and included hundreds of people who had illegally listed a UPS box as their residence.[25]

That same year Broward County allowed a convicted felon to put his name on the ballot,[26] though votes for him were not counted since he was ineligible to hold office.[27] Dr. Snipes supports restoring voting rights to former felons,[28] but in this case, the convicted felon had not had his rights to vote or hold office restored (though he claimed to have been voting since 1996).

Dr. Snipes remained a controversial figure, ordering a possibly unnecessary reelection in 2015,[29] releasing the results of a local election in August 2016—when Snipes herself was up for reelection—half-an-hour before the polls closed,[30] printing 173,000 ballots with a typo that might confuse some voters,[31] and destroying ballots that were the subject of litigation.[32]

She also suffered another embarrassment with absentee ballots in 2016, when a temporary worker, Chelsey Marie Smith, witnessed four officials in a room filling out what she reported to be blank ballots.[33] Ms. Smith was fired the next day, and an investigation was launched. Dr. Snipes said the officials were merely making ballot duplicates for faxed military ballots, and though questions remained about the incident, the investigation was closed.[34]

All of these issues prompted the American Civil Rights Union, a Virginia-based nonprofit, to file a federal lawsuit in 2017. The group asked U.S. District Judge Beth Bloom to order the county to improve the integrity of its voter rolls.

In court, Snipes acknowledged that her office had made mistakes and that some noncitizens and felons had voted illegally. But Snipes said her office wanted to ensure that eligible voters were not removed from the rolls by mistake.[35]

But in Broward County, as in many other counties across the country, voting rolls seem suspiciously full of mistakes; and many of the people charged with fixing them don't seem all that interested in doing so.

Double-Barreled Voter Fraud

Even today, Kansas and Missouri are quintessentially American places. Baseball, barbeque, and Budweiser beer are alive and well, served with Midwestern charm and quiet virtues. It's the land of Mark Twain, the Mississippi River, and the Kansas City Royals.

But there are the shadows of a dark past, of "Bleeding Kansas" and the vicious border fights in the 1850s over whether the new state of Kansas would be a slave state or a free state. Those pre–Civil War fights included aggressive, blatant vote fraud by pro-slavery men from Missouri, crossing the border to vote illegally in Kansas's first elections.

In 2004, on the 150th anniversary of the Kansas-Nebraska Act, which officially created the Kansas Territory, the *Kansas City Star* decided to investigate whether Kansans and Missourians were still crossing borders to vote or otherwise voting illegally.[1]

They found at least three hundred illegal double votes across state lines and within the state of Missouri. A sister paper, the *Billings Gazette*, noted that "The exact number is impossible to determine because many counties have shredded their poll books, as allowed under state law, and state computer files are rife with data errors."[2]

The paper's analysis compared the voter registration rolls in both states for exact matches of names and birth dates. While the technique showed fraud, it was hardly comprehensive. It could only pinpoint voters who made no attempt to conceal their identity. It did not address how many illegal voters might have voted under assumed names. "Election officials said the findings show that the voting system is vulnerable to fraud and that it's a particularly serious threat in a time of razor-thin election margins."[3]

The findings were consistent with what other media outlets were finding across the country. A *New York Daily News* analysis found forty-six thousand people who were registered to vote in both Florida and New York, with between four hundred and a thousand of them voting in the 2000 election in both states.[4] Remember that the presidential election in 2000 was decided by a mere 537 votes in Florida. The *Orlando Sentinel* found sixty-eight thousand people registered in both Florida and either Georgia or North Carolina, with 1,650 of them voting in two states from 2000 to 20002.[5]

A more recent case shows how the problem persists. In 2016, a man in Wyandotte County, Kansas, on the Missouri border, was charged with taking advantage of early voting, and then voting again on election day in the same election.[6] In 2014, he allegedly voted on both sides of the Kansas-Missouri border.

"The crime of double voting seems to be a crime of opportunity," Kansas Secretary of State Kris Kobach told KCTV5 News regarding the station's Wyandotte County report. "An individual discovers he or she is still registered in another state and thinks, maybe is tempted, maybe says 'I can vote in both states and get away with it'."[7]

In Oregon, a local newspaper found that a former county commission candidate had allegedly voted for years in both Washington state and Oregon.[8] The former elected official was one of at least seventy-four potential double voting cases, covering five states, discovered by a study of ballots cast in the 2016 general election.[9]

If that seems low, it might be because verifying voter fraud that crosses state lines depends on state and local authorities gathering such evidence—and as political scientists Ray Christensen and Thomas J. Shultz note, "perhaps only the worst attempts of election fraud leave behind such evidence."[10]

The bottom line is that voting twice is illegal, yet it happens all the time, across the country, and is rarely punished.

In February 2017, Michigan's outgoing elections director, Chris Thomas, announced 31 instances of double votes in the November 2016 general elections, with individuals apparently voting by absentee ballot and again at the polls. Six months later, not a single arrest or prosecution materialized. After three years, such cases can no longer be prosecuted.[11]

Colorado's secretary of state said in September 2017 that forty-eight people were under investigation in his state for double-voting.[12]

In Tennessee, half a dozen people were found to have double-voted at a single polling station in Davidson County in 2014.[13] Two years earlier, a Tennessee man was reported to have voted three times in three different states.[14]

"It's too easy to vote twice, it comes down to your honor," said Jay DeLancy, executive director of a North Carolina volunteer group called The Voting Integrity Project.[15] The Voting Integrity Project discovered the Tennessee triple voter. "It's a lot more widespread than people think because the general public thinks there is no voter fraud. As proof they look at prosecutions, but we have learned how difficult it is to get prosecutions," he said.

A nonprofit election watchdog known as the Virginia Voting Alliance forwarded 164 cases of potential double votes to elections officials in both Maryland and Virginia after the 2012 presidential election.[16] The cases spanned neighboring locations in Washington, D.C., Maryland, and Fairfax County, Virginia.

"We are concerned that these voters are going to be able to continue to do this until they are prosecuted," Cathy Kelleher, spokesperson for watchdog group Election Integrity Maryland told the *Baltimore Sun*.

Of these 164 potential cases, elections officials pursued only seventeen. Even the *Baltimore Sun* editorial board, which rejected voter fraud as a meaningful issue, admitted "the chances that such incidents will result in fraud convictions are slim."[17]

"We've argued before that the Maryland Office of State Prosecutor, the agency responsible for prosecuting such cases in this state, has too often been reluctant to investigate irregularities with its admittedly limited resources," the *Sun's* editors wrote.

Significant penalties do exist for those convicted of double-voting—in Florida, for example, one count of voter fraud carries a maximum penalty of five years in prison and a $5,000 fine.[18] The problem is a lack of effective oversight and enforcement that would make these penalties mean something.

In 2017, the nonprofit Government Accountability Institute tried to provide some oversight by investigating duplicate voting in the 2016 general election. Interestingly, no government or private entity looks for double-voting across all fifty states. States are not required to compare their voter rolls, though recently some states have joined data-sharing programs such as the Electronic Registration Information Center (ERIC) and the Interstate Voter Registration Crosscheck Program.

ERIC helps twenty-two states and the District of Columbia improve the accuracy of their voter rolls, and the program is designed to increase voter registration, rather than identify voter fraud.[19]

According to leaked Open Society Foundation documents, ERIC was partially seeded with grant money from the George Soros network.[20] The Interstate Voter Registration Crosscheck Program was founded by a Republican, Kansas Secretary of State Kobach, and counted thirty member states as of 2017. The initiative was created to prevent voters from registering in more than one state.[21]

While the Interstate Voter Registration Crosscheck Program is no doubt tackling the issue, the GAI investigation is the largest double-voting study to date. It was impossible to get the relevant voting roll information from all fifty states, but GAI did obtain voter roll data from twenty-one states: Arkansas, California, Connecticut, Florida, Iowa, Kansas, Maryland, Missouri, Montana, Nebraska, New Jersey, New York, Oklahoma, Oregon, Pennsylvania, Rhode Island, South Carolina, Tennessee, Texas, Washington, and West Virginia. That amounts to about 17 percent of possible state-to-state comparisons

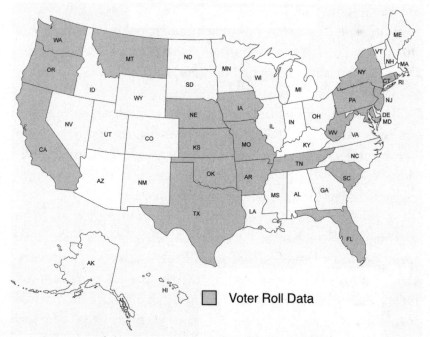

Courtesy of the Government Accountability Institute.

Using strict statistical guidelines, GAI found 8,471 highly likely cases of illegal duplicate voting.[22] In July 2017, Kobach, then the vice-chair of the Presidential Commission on Election Integrity, endorsed GAI's findings during a national radio interview. He said that the number of double votes "seems right in line with kind of numbers we're seeing among the thirty states in the Interstate Cross Check Program."[23] The GAI report also found more than fifteen thousand voter registrations which listed addresses that were either illegal for voter registration, such as a PO Box, or clearly fraudulent, such as a vacant lot, abandoned building, basketball court, and so on. The report found 45,880 votes that were cast by people whose dates of birth meant they were at least 115 years old before the 2016 general election. (For the record, the oldest living person in the United States is 113 years old.)[24]

After the razor-thin presidential election of 2000—decided by 537 ballot votes and five Electoral College votes[25]—Congress enacted reforms that were meant to strengthen voter identity verification. The legislation was called the Help America Vote Act (HAVA) of 2002.[26] It passed Congress with overwhelming bipartisan support and was signed into law by the election's winner, President George W. Bush.

One of the Act's reforms was a requirement that eligible voters use authoritative forms of identification when registering to vote. Valid driver's license numbers and the last four digits of an individual's Social Security number were now required for all new voter registrants. Pre-HAVA registered voters are exempt.

Yet the law also allows for other forms of identification to be accepted, with some being far less reliable than others. Alternative forms of identification include state ID cards, passports, military IDs, employee IDs, and student IDs. They also allow bank statements, utility bills, or pay stubs. States can also offer additional identification options. If the alternative forms of ID seem to undermine the point of requiring a driver's license or Social Security number, it's because they do.

In Rhode Island, taken as a sample case, GAI found that more than 30 percent of voters in the 2016 general election did not register to vote using either a Social Security number or driver's license number. The federal HAVA law requires anyone registering for the first time after January 1, 2003, to provide a driver's license number or a Social Security number. But GAI found 22,389 cases of voters in Rhode Island who first registered after that date without using that type of identification.[27] In total, nearly *one-third* of Rhode Island voters are registered with an ID that cannot be definitively verified using the information contained in the state's voter registration system.

To illustrate the absurdity of the state and local election safeguards, GAI's technical partner in the study, Simpatico Software Systems, presented the Rhode Island secretary of state's office with the following scenario:

If a voter registration form was submitted by an individual with the name John Jacob Jingleheimer Schmidt, a birthdate of 1/1/1970, a residential address that was clearly a commercial office building, no driver's license, no Social Security number, and the registration form was sent to the appropriate elections office by mail, would this application be approved and added to the Rhode Island state voter roll?

The Rhode Island secretary of state's office said 'yes,' while noting that registration oversight in Rhode Island is performed at the local level.

Per the secretary of state's office, local elections officials would send a letter via the U.S. Postal Service to the address provided on the voter registration application. If the letter was not returned as undeliverable, then the applicant is duly registered and no further checks would be performed, unless the registration was challenged by a person or entity outside of government.

If the letter were returned as undeliverable, or if the improperly listed commercial business were to return the letter with a postal comment that the registering individual did not live at that address, then the application would be put on hold.

With the application placed on hold, the potential voter would still need to provide a photo ID at his polling place, but it would not have to be a driver's license; it could even be a gym membership or a company (even fictitious) photo ID. Even without providing an ID, he could cast a provisional ballot; because his name would be on the voting rolls, he could not legally be turned away. His provisional ballot, pursuant to Rhode Island's voter ID laws, would then be counted after nothing more rigorous than an election worker deciding that the ballot signature matched the signature on the voter ID card that every voter is given before voting.

To say that this is a system ripe for fraud is to say the obvious, but the vulnerabilities GAI found in Rhode Island's voter registration system are shared by many states. Without requiring a person to present verifiable identification during registration, there's simply no way to confirm a voter's identity or citizenship status.

Worse, whistleblowers can easily become wrongdoers to those supposedly guarding election integrity. If a group like GAI suspected names on Rhode Island's voter rolls were fraudulent, and alerted state officials to that fact, the group would have to file an official "voter challenge," which carries the risk of a criminal penalty if proven wrong.

The state statute reads: "Every person who willfully and maliciously challenges the registration of a voter without reasonable cause to suspect that the voter is not qualified shall be guilty of a misdemeanor and shall, in addition, be liable to the challenged voter for compensatory and punitive damages as well as for his or her counsel fees."[28]

The practical effect is to make it risky to question possibly improper voter registrations. And right now, it appears that many states' safeguards against false registrations and double-voting are sorely in need of an upgrade.

CHAPTER

Who Counts the Votes?

hree days before the 1996 elections, Bill Clinton was poised to win re-election over Kansas Senator Bob Dole. In Nebraska, Ben Nelson, the state's popular governor, was in a virtual dead-heat with millionaire businessman Chuck Hagel for a U.S. Senate seat. Nelson had won the governor's race two years earlier by a landslide and seemed a good bet to keep the Senate seat in Democrat control, since no Republican had won it in eighteen years. The polls, however, were close. Three days before the election, a poll from the *Omaha World-Herald* showed a deadlock, with each candidate getting 47 percent support. The Gallup polling organization was on record as saying, "We can't predict the outcome."

So, when Chuck Hagel won by fifteen points, it was, as *Harper's* noted, "enough to raise eyebrows across the nation."[1]

What few realized at the time of the election was that Hagel owned millions of dollars' worth of stock in the parent company of American Information Systems, whose voting machines would count his own votes in November of 2016. In fact, Hagel had been chairman of AIS until just two weeks before election night, and his campaign treasurer, Michael McCarthy, was the parent company's founder.

Senator Hagel's ties to the company responsible for counting the votes in Nebraska elections didn't fully come to light until six years later, when his opponent in his bid for re-election made them a campaign issue. Charlie Matulka asked for a hand count of the ballots in his race, in which he received only 70,290 votes, or less than a fifth of the total number of the registered Democrats in the state. Matulka's request was denied because, under Nebraska law, recounts must be conducted using the same "vote-counting device" the votes were cast with—in this case the optical scanners manufactured by Hagel's former company.

Nebraska Democrats' suspicion of the validity of Hagel's win via electronic voting machines underscores the inherent problems that come with voting systems that lack a paper trail. This places huge responsibility—and power—in the hands of local elections officials.

Good elections officers today must ensure that all eligible voters are able to vote while they do everything possible to prevent ineligible voters from doing so. Elections supervisors have increasingly taken on the role of an IT manager, becoming both reliant on and responsible for the technology that manages their voter rolls and ballot counting.

In 1964, Orange County, California, became the first jurisdiction to use optical scan voting machines. But it was only after the 2000 presidential election, with the infamous "hanging chads" on Florida's paper ballots, that Congress allocated $2 billion to help states transition to more technically advanced voting machines.[2]

As with most early adoptions of new technology, there were issues along the way. Computers were now counting the votes, but not everyone knew exactly what was happening with the computers.

In November 2004, Jefferson Knight was a Florida Republican Party volunteer, running its Miami-Dade County command center during the election between president George W. Bush and Democrat Senator John Kerry. After the previous close election, and with the sitting president's brother running Florida, all eyes were watching the Sunshine State for the slightest irregularities.

On Election Day, Knight got a call from a Republican Party poll watcher serving a predominantly Republican precinct in the south Miami area. She told Knight that every few minutes the line of voters was being stopped. Voters were becoming frustrated and angry; some were going home.

The line stoppages were happening because one Democratic Party poll watcher and one Kerry campaign poll watcher had convinced the clerk in charge of the precinct that it was crucially important for all vote totals at the end of the day to be equal on each machine. They persuaded precinct officials to stop voting periodically, the Republican poll watcher reported, so the machines could be moved around within the precinct[3], to "get the votes to be even on each machine."

Knight, a lawyer and longtime elections observer, characterized the logic succinctly: "That's horseshit!" he told the Republican poll watcher. "Tell that clerk to get that line moving. These people are stopping the flow of voters, and it's wrong."

Whether the real explanation for the bizarre demand was ignorance or attempted obstruction, there was no reason the precinct's voting machines had to have the same number of ballots. Our understanding of the strengths and weaknesses of computer voting systems has improved a great deal since then. Unfortunately, the actual technology in electronic voting systems hasn't.

The problem is that while technology keeps advancing, voting machines aren't keeping up—in fact, they're falling apart.

An analysis by the left-leaning Brennan Center estimated that in 2016, fourteen states used voting machines that were fifteen years old. "No one expects a laptop to last for 10 years," said Lawrence Norden, deputy director of the Brennan Center's Democracy Program. "How can we expect these machines, many of which were designed and engineered in the 1990s, to keep running without increased failures?"[4]

We are already at that point, all across the nation.

In 2017, Plainview County Clerk Latrice Kemp requested that her Texas county's voting machines, in use since 2005, be replaced.

"They've been great, but more problems are cropping up each time we use them," Kemp told commissioners. "During our last election, we had two polling locations where we had static screens when we turned them on." And she warned, "As our current machines grow older, we expect support will be going away because they are obsolete."[5]

In the 2016 general election, Wayne County, Michigan, found that one-third of its precincts had problems with ballots.

"It's not good," conceded Daniel Baxter, elections director for the city of Detroit, the seat of Wayne County.

Baxter blamed the city's decade-old voting machines, saying eighty-seven optical scanners broke on Election Day. Many jammed when voters fed ballots into scanners, and if ballots were re-fed multiple times it could have resulted in multiple votes if poll workers failed to adjust the counters.[6]

In York County, Pennsylvania, election machine problems meant a voter could pick the same candidate twice, giving them an extra vote.[7]

In Washington County, Utah, only a quarter of the county's voting machines had properly programmed memory cards, which meant that some voters were turned away when they tried to vote in the 2016 presidential election.[8]

In North Carolina, the NAACP sent a letter to the state's board of elections after voters complained that machines had flipped votes in five counties. The group noted that, in each case, the voter was able to correct the error before the ballot was cast. But it asked the board to remove malfunctioning machines and to post signs reminding voters to check their ballots before submitting them.[9]

Some people see these problems as a deliberate attempt to rig elections. Lawrence Norden of the Brennan Center doesn't agree.

"If you were actually trying to rig an election, it would be a very stupid thing to do, to let the voter know that you were doing it," he said.

Norden thinks the real problem is that too many voting machines rely on outdated technology; and the hardware itself is starting to wear out. "Over time, as people vote," explains Norden, the calibration on the touch screens "becomes less and less accurate." By the end of a long day of voting, the machines aren't as accurate as they were in the morning; and, over time, the screens can become seriously misaligned.[10]

That's natural wear and tear on the machines, but there are other vulnerabilities based on the design rather than the age of the machines. Nearly every make and model of digital voting machine has been shown to be vulnerable to hacking.[11]

In one case, several Pennsylvania voters reported an electronic voting machine had "flipped" their votes. When they selected their desired candidate on a digital touch-screen, the machine selected a different candidate. The incident was first thought to be a technical error (such as the calibration problem), but upon review it was discovered that remote-access software had been installed, allowing the machine to be controlled from another location.

"Logs showed the software was installed two years earlier and used multiple times, most notably for 80 minutes on November 1, 2010, the night before a federal election," the *New York Times* reported.[12] "The software, it turns out, was being used not by a hacker, but by an authorized county contractor working from home. Still, the arrangement meant that anyone who might gain control of the contractor's home computer could use it to access and gain control of the county's election system."[13]

It's an example of what many experts cited by the *New York Times* already suspected—that election systems throughout the country are poorly secured.

That stunning assessment was driven home at a gathering of hackers and computer security specialists at the annual DEF CON conference in July 2017. Amid concerns of Russian hacking in the 2016 presidential election, conference attendees set out to determine whether electronic voting machines and state voter registration databases could be vulnerable to cyberattacks. The result? Many systems were penetrated with relatively little effort. In one instance, a sixteen-year-old boy reportedly hacked a voting machine in forty-five minutes.[14]

A year later, NBC News reported that Russian hackers did, in fact, penetrate the election infrastructure of seven states.[15] Relying on anonymous "intelligence community" sources, the network said hackers either entered state websites or voter roll databases, but no votes were changed and no voters were taken off the rolls.

The only good news is that state election officials seem to be waking up, slowly, to the vulnerabilities of obsolete electronic voting machines. In December 2017, U.S. Senator James Lankford of Oklahoma introduced the Secure Elections Act, which would give states 386 million dollars' worth of federal grants to improve their election systems. But as of this writing that bill had yet to receive a committee hearing.[16]

North Carolina has taken action on its own—not by modernizing its digital machines, but by pledging to return to paper ballots by 2019.[17]

Angus King, U.S. Senator from Maine, has repeatedly sounded the alarm over the vulnerability of electronic voting machines. King asked officials in the Senate Appropriations Committee for $160 million to help states replace voting machines that don't provide paper backups, and to perform post-election audits to compare electronic records with physical evidence. The response from his Senate colleagues? "It didn't go anywhere," King said.[18]

The irony is that even if states had the ability to audit their results, not all of them would. Only two states require a full post-election audit of all votes cast. Most states settle for verifying fewer than half the votes through an audit. Full recounts generally occur only if there is a contested election result, and not always then. The rules for an automatic recount vary widely from state to state. For example, in Arizona and Florida there is no provision for candidates requesting a recount. In Arizona, a recount is triggered if the candidates are separated by only a small number of votes (the precise number depending on the number of votes cast, but generally a margin of 0.1 percent). Then 5 percent of the precincts are randomly selected and recounted. If that recount does not push a candidate over the necessary margin of victory, then 10 percent of the precincts are selected, and another recount is conducted. If that too fails to extend the margin, then all the precincts are recounted.[19] In Florida, a recount is triggered if the difference in candidates' vote totals is less than 0.5 percent.[20]

In Idaho, candidates request recounts by precinct. In Iowa, officials audit a number of random precincts chosen by state commissioner after every general election.[21] In Louisiana, any voter or candidate can file a request in writing for a recount of absentee and early voting ballots, if those ballots represent the victory margin of an election.[22]

In Michigan, a recount rule temporarily deprived the eventual winner, Ronald Lee Miller, from taking the oath of office. Officials in Wayne County admitted that in their rush to certify the election they had failed to count dozens of votes, which would have made Miller the victor over his opponent.

But Wayne County refused to alter the results.

Why? Officials said Miller failed to request a recount within six days, as is required by state law. The county interpreted the law to include the four days its offices were closed for Thanksgiving.

It took eight months, a recount, and a lawsuit for Miller to be declared the winner.

One would like to think that stories like that of Ronald Lee Miller in Wayne County are a rare exception. But it is jarring to learn that the Election Integrity Project, a joint international venture of Harvard University and the University of Sydney, ranked the integrity of American elections on a par with those of Argentina, Mongolia, and Rwanda.[23] While the Election Integrity Project's criteria might have been imperfect—it went beyond problems with ballots to cover campaign finance and other issues—it gives added meaning to a dictum commonly attributed to Joseph Stalin: "I consider it completely unimportant who in the party will vote, or how; but what is extraordinarily important is this—who will count the votes, and how."

America needs to do better.

CHAPTER

9

Who Cares Who Votes?

It's important to know who is voting in our elections. If for no other reason, a fraudulent or ineligible vote cancels out an honest vote. Such an occurrence ought to be unacceptable, yet there's a confounding resistance to ensuring against it.

Alan Schulkin, head of New York City's Board of Elections in 2016, expressed that concern as well as any American voter: "I take my vote seriously, and I don't want 10 other people coming in negating my vote by voting for the other candidate when they aren't even registered voters."[1]

Schulkin's remarks were caught on camera by an undercover Project Veritas reporter, who asked him whether voter fraud exists. "Certain neighborhoods in particular, they bus people around to vote," he said. "They put them in a bus and go poll site to poll site." Asked if he meant black and Hispanic neighborhoods, Schulkin nodded: "Yeah, and Chinese, too."[2]

The off-the-record admission became public one month before the 2016 presidential election. Rather than investigate or implement measures to crack down on the voter fraud activities described by the chairman of the city's Board of Elections, Mayor Bill de Blasio, a Clinton supporter, called for Schulkin, a fellow Democrat, to resign.[3]

While the vast majority of voters are honest, gaming the system isn't difficult—even in states with voter ID laws. It's hard to imagine many elections officials don't know this, especially since they help make the rules.

In North Dakota, a potential voter does not even have to register prior to Election Day. Each precinct is responsible for ensuring that voters are North Dakota residents who have resided in their precinct for at least thirty days—and a North Dakota driver's license or an ID issued by a tribal government (a form of identification issued by the secretary of state) can cover that.[4]

North Dakota's laws are not that far from the norm. Rhode Island's voter ID law is called a "non-strict non-photo ID" law, and that's what more than a quarter of all states have; fully one-third of states have no ID requirement at all; and only eight states carry a "strict photo ID" requirement.

The lack of strict voter ID requirements nationwide is a hindrance to ensuring election integrity. But politics is an even bigger hurdle. The issue of voter fraud has become so partisan that many states outright refuse to participate in any independent review of their voter rolls.

"How can we ensure against voter fraud if states won't release their data?" said Ken Block of the data analytics company Simpatico Software Systems, who testified at the opening meeting of President Trump's bipartisan election integrity commission in September 2017.

The commission attempted to address many of the same problems identified in the Government Accountability Institute report on double-voting. But even with presidential authority, the commission could not obtain the voter rolls of all fifty states to conduct a full analytical review of recent federal elections.

Block said the commission was well-intentioned but flawed from the outset. It was supposed to be a bipartisan advisory body, but the governing structure allowed for Republicans and Democrats to fight each other into grinding the commission to a halt.

Its biggest mistake, Block explained, was in immediately seeking voters' driver's license numbers and Social Security numbers. "That's protected information," he said. That made it too easy for partisan opponents to resist otherwise reasonable voter roll data requests, he said. "I understand why they did it, because it would make cleaning up voter rolls easy as pie. If you don't have it, you have to jump through hoops to verify any reasonable findings."

To see just how fraught the process of obtaining voter roll data has become consider this: Kris Kobach was both the secretary of state for Kansas and the appointed vice-chair of the election integrity commission; yet Secretary of State Kris Kobach couldn't legally provide Kris Kobach of the election integrity commission with the confidential voter roll information he was requesting from his own state.[5]

Maine Secretary of State Matthew Dunlap, a Democrat, also served on the commission—and *sued* it. Dunlap alleged that the commission denied him the same documents and communications as other commission members, and that it was insufficiently reflecting "a diversity of viewpoints." Dunlap asserted in his federal lawsuit that he had been left out of meetings where agendas were set and decisions were made.[6]

But there was a good reason for that, according to J. Christian Adams, a fellow commission member and an attorney who had worked in the Department of Justice Voting Rights Division under presidents George W. Bush and Barack Obama.

"What was going on was there were people from the commission, one in particular—the Secretary of State of Maine, Matthew

Dunlap—who simply did not want the commission to do its work," Adams said.[7] "He was sort of on a crusade to satisfy the radical progressives who don't want any discussion about voter fraud. If you even ask the questions, if you attempt to quantify the problem or do anything about it, these interest groups go completely berserk, and they lose their mind."[8]

Adams said he would email commission members and within an hour his email would be leaked to the liberal-leaning news media.

"What happened was [Dunlap] took the role of saboteur. He didn't want anything done. He sued the commission. He disagreed with the premise [of the commission and asserted] that there wasn't anything wrong and that's how things rolled," Adams concluded.[9]

In December 2017, a federal district judge ruled that the commission needed to provide Dunlap better access to commission documents moving forward.[10] Dunlap and his supporters claimed victory. The same month, the U.S. Court of Appeals for the D.C. Circuit shot down a separate lawsuit lodged by a group with funding ties to George Soros.[11] The commission was eventually sued into oblivion by the administration's political opponents. In all, eighteen lawsuits or legal actions were brought against the national election integrity effort.[12] (A list can be found on the Brennan Center's website.)[13]

In January 2018, President Trump disbanded the commission.[14]

In 2017, after the GAI double-voting report exposed thousands of unreported cases of double-voting, with Rhode Island as a case study, the Rhode Island secretary of state's office did something peculiar: it redacted full birthdates from the state's publicly available voter roll. Without full birthdates, GAI's double-voting experiment cannot be replicated. Curiously, the decision was said to be made in the interests of election integrity.

"Rhode Island Secretary of State Nellie Gorbea has pledged to safeguard the privacy of Rhode Island voters and the integrity of Rhode Island's election systems," wrote Rob Rock, the state Director of Elections, in an email to Ken Block on August 3, 2017.

Rock said the Rhode Island Department of State was acting on behalf of concerned state residents, and therefore decided to remove the month and day of birth from all public reports generated from the state's Central Voter Registration System, despite the CVRS having provided voters' full dates of birth since its inception.

In the email exchange, Block told Rock, "This does nothing to protect individual confidentiality," and explained that an individual's birth date typically can be obtained through a simple Google search. Redacting that information from a publicly available voter roll only serves to inhibit accountability, he said.

"Without a full date of birth, the kind of (double vote) matching we have done is no longer possible, which is NOT a step forward to transparency in Rhode Island elections," Block said.

But other investigative efforts weren't so easily foiled.

Block and GAI submitted a list of 224 voters who had cast ballots in the 2016 presidential election but registered to vote using clearly fraudulent or prohibited addresses to the Rhode Island Board of Elections.[15] Had GAI pursued the matter and demanded that the state verify that these people were legally registered, GAI itself could, under state law, have been sued for questioning someone's right to vote. So instead of challenging the voters' registrations, Block asked that the Board send the list to local Boards of Canvassers. The Boards can check improper voter addresses by sending an official letter asking that the addresses be confirmed.

Of the 224 letters sent, the Boards received 109 responses, which includes letters returned as undeliverable by the postal service. Roughly 7 percent of all respondents canceled their voter registrations, and nearly half subsequently changed their addresses.

"In some cases, we were able to determine that some of these voters did not have residences in Rhode Island, and in other cases the voter changed their address to a residential address in a different Rhode Island municipality," Block explained. "In either scenario, that voter was using an improper address to cast a ballot in a jurisdiction where that voter was not legally allowed to vote," he said.

Result	% of 109 respondents	% of 224 identified voters
Voter changed address	44%	21%
Mailing was undeliverable to voter	11%	5%
Voter cancelled their registration	7%	3.5%
Clerical error in address	2.7%	1.3%
Voter claimed residence at questionable address, like a storage unit	24%	12%
Voter is homeless	5.5%	2.6%

Email correspondence from Ken Block.

If results like these could be found in the country's smallest state, what confidence should any of us have that similar errors and fraud aren't larger, more politically valuable states—like California?

In September 2017, Block filed a complaint with the U.S. Department of Justice alleging that Rhode Island election officials were committing major election law violations,[16] including failing to abide by the voter identification requirements of the federal Help American Vote Act.[17] Block found that Rhode Island performed the mandated ID verification only for voters who registered by mail. The law, however, requires verification of *all* new voters, matching the driver's licenses or Social Security numbers on their voter registration applications with the information on file at the Department of Motor Vehicles or the Social Security Administration.

"We need to know who voters are," Block said in an interview. "For example, we need to be able to remove people from voter rolls when they die."

Block discovered that an astounding 30 percent of Rhode Island's 2016 general election votes were cast by individuals who did not register to vote with either a driver's license or Social Security number. Put another way, nearly one in three voters do not have strong identifying information in the state's voter registration system. The finding was confirmed by the secretary of state's office:

From: Rob Rock [mailto:rrock@sos.ri.gov]
Sent: Wednesday, April 26, 2017 1:54 PM
To: 'Ken Block' <kblock@simpaticosoftware.com>
Subject: RE: Checking in on my request

Ken,
Below are the numbers you requested. I don't believe that anyone who registered before the Help America Vote Act would have their DL or SS information in our system. Also, before the voter ID law took effect, anyone who did not have a DL or SS on file would have had to show ID before voting. Now, everyone must show ID.

Rob

VOTERS COUNTS WITH NO DMV ID AND SSN	
TOTAL COUNT	CURRENT_VOTER_STATUS
217383	Active
5325	Active with NCOA Change
7670	Inactive
159	Pending
Total Voters : 230,537	

Total voters who voted in November 2016 Presidential election and don't have SSN and DMV are **143806.**

Rob Rock
Director of Elections
RI Department of State | Secretary of State Nellie M. Gorbea
Email: rrock@sos.ri.gov | Website: www.sos.ri.gov | Twitter: @RISecState
148 W. River Street, Providence RI 02904 | 401-222-2340

Our Mission: The Rhode Island Department of State engages and empowers all Rhode Islanders by making government more accessible and transparent, encouraging civic pride, enhancing commerce and ensuring that elections are fair, fast and accurate.

Email correspondence from Ken Block.

More than 22,000 recent presidential election voters were allowed to register without providing the ID mandated by federal law. The highest percentage of those 22,000 voters came from Central Falls—an area where 38 percent of the population is listed as "foreign born" by the U.S. Census.[18] According to Block's analysis, about 21 percent of 2016 Central Falls general election voters did not supply a driver's license or Social Security number after the HAVA law mandated it.

All Voters Registered After 1/1/2003 Voting Without PII

Personally Identifying Information (PII) e.g. driver's license or SSN is not in the voter registration system as mandated by federal law.

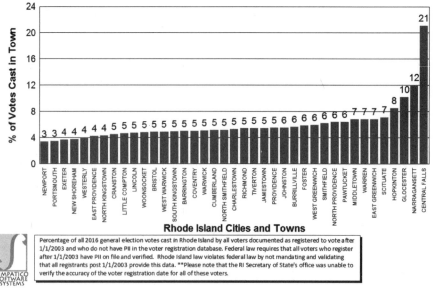

Percentage of all 2016 general election votes cast in Rhode Island by all voters documented as registered to vote after 1/1/2003 and who do not have PII in the voter registration database. Federal law requires that all voters who register after 1/1/2003 have PII on file and verified. Rhode Island law violates federal law by not mandating and validating that all registrants post 1/1/2003 provide this data. **Please note that the RI Secretary of State's office was unable to verify the accuracy of the voter registration date for all of these voters.

Email correspondence from Ken Block.

But what's even more troubling is that Rhode Island followed the HAVA requirements until shortly before the 2008 presidential election.[19]

"Upon their original adoption in 2003, the State's registration rules did not violate HAVA. An August 2008 Rule change, only two months ahead of the 2008 General Election, appears to begin Rhode Island's pattern of HAVA violations. The impact of this rule change was an unprecedented explosion of voters who registered to vote without personally identifying information in the two months before the 2008 elections," the federal complaint says.

The 2008 administrative rule change allowing people to register to vote without HAVA-required identification occurred under former Rhode Island Secretary of State Ralph Mollis and former Executive Director of the state Board of Elections Robert Kando. Mollis was a donor to Democratic politicians—including Congressman Patrick J. Kennedy, U.S. Senator Jack Reed, and Hillary Clinton[20]—and Kando, who had previously been fired as deputy clerk at the Rhode Island District Court, was twice suspended as executive director of the state Board of Elections, before being fired from that job in August 2016.[21]

Kando was hired as the Board's executive director in 2005, amid allegations that he was not qualified for the job. According to the *Providence Journal,* he did not have "practical work experience in areas of voter registration, conduct of elections, state and federal election laws and campaign finance." The previous executive director had himself pleaded no contest to three felony counts of obtaining money under false pretenses.[22]

Block's federal complaint questioned whether Rhode Island's state election officials "intentionally or ignorantly ran afoul of HAVA."

Rhode Island is not the only state to have veered away from HAVA. In 2006, the Department of Justice filed a complaint against New Jersey for almost the exact same violations.[23] On the day the New Jersey DOJ complaint was filed, the state agreed to correct its violations.[24] The DOJ also demanded New Jersey update its voter registration records to account for tens of thousands of voters who were registered with no viable birth date.

New Jersey seems to have complied, but with a twist. GAI's 2017 report on double-voting identified 31,260 New Jersey general election voters who registered to vote using birthdates of "1/1/1800," raising suspicions that obviously wrong date was used as a default date for voter registrations that were accepted without providing an actual date of birth.

Similarly, with regard to Rhode Island, Block's DOJ complaint demands that state officials backfill missing required identifying information for the hundreds of thousands of incomplete voter registrations.

"Without personally-identifying information in the voter registration data, it is exceedingly difficult for Rhode Island to conform to HAVA requirements to remove deceased voters from the voter registration system, not to mention maintain Rhode Island's voter registration data—the bedrock of the state's election system," he said.

By mid-November 2017, Rhode Island's Board of Elections had ordered a draft regulation to eliminate the ID loophole for would-be voters.[25] This amounts to a victory—albeit a small one, in the smallest state of the Union. Other states almost certainly face the same issues. But as Ken Block's Rhode Island investigation and indeed the Presidential Commission on Election Integrity show, opponents of election reform await at every turn with the threat of a lawsuit or criminal charges.

The integrity of voting rolls is nationwide problem that needs to be addressed at the federal level, either by the Department of Justice or the Department of Homeland Security.

10

Summing Up: Voting and Citizenship

There is no doubt that American elections are tainted—even won and lost—by illegal voting. And the sad reality is that many of our governing officials don't care. Some even condone it.

Now, consider the fight currently taking place over the 2020 Census.

Citing a need to better enforce the Voting Rights Act, the Trump Justice Department has restored a question to the 2020 Census, asking whether respondents are U.S. citizens. This has enraged Democrats. Nineteen state attorneys general, including those of California, New York, Illinois, and Pennsylvania, wrote letters of protest to Commerce Secretary Wilbur Ross, whose department oversees the taking of the Census, claiming that the question "would significantly depress participation, causing a population undercount that would disproportionately harm states and cities with large immigrant communities."[1]

Xavier Becerra, California's attorney general, has threatened "to take all necessary and legal action to protect a full and accurate Census."

"This is clearly an attempt to bully and discourage our immigrant communities from participating in the 2020 Census count," Becerra said in a statement.[2]

"We also call on Congress to fully and immediately fund preparations for the 2020 Census. California simply has too much to lose for us to allow the Trump Administration to botch this important decennial obligation."

Becerra and the other protesting attorneys general are incensed because while noncitizens cannot legally vote in federal elections, they can still alter the balance of representation in Congress and potentially determine the outcome of presidential elections.[3]

Every ten years, the 435 seats in the House of Representatives are reapportioned based on population figures gathered by the U.S. Census Bureau. Noncitizens are included in the population data. This inclusion is based on an interpretation of the Fourteenth Amendment's provision that "whole number of persons in each state" should be counted for purposes of representation. The Fourteenth Amendment was written, of course, to ensure the rights of newly freed slaves, not illegal immigrants; the very next phrase of Section 2 specifically and tellingly excludes the counting of "Indians not taxed." Counting the "whole number of persons" is how the Census has always been conducted. Still, the citizenship data is valuable, and important for election integrity.

According to the Department of Homeland Security, nearly 1.2 million lawful permanent residents were admitted into the United States in 2016, and more than a million were admitted in each of the prior two years.[4] That's in addition to the estimated 11.1 million illegal immigrants living mostly in dense urban areas, particularly in California and Northeastern cities. A Pew Research study reported that "unauthorized immigrants tend to live where other immigrants live,"[5] which is highly significant because, in terms of the Census, this gives states a perverse incentive to pursue "sanctuary" policies that welcome and encourage illegal immigration.

Professor Leonard Steinhorn pointed out in the *Washington Post* that even without voting, noncitizens could tip the balance in a close general election because, just as their inclusion in the Census inflates a state's population, so too does it inflate that state's number of electoral votes.[6] California, now a sanctuary state, is the biggest beneficiary of extra federal representation. Using 2010 Census data—and the number of immigrants, legal and illegal, has grown dramatically since then—Steinhorn calculated that California would lose five House seats and New York and Washington State would each lose one congressional seat without their noncitizen populations. In other words, noncitizens in Washington and New York offset the voting power in the House of Representatives of the citizens of Alaska, Montana, North Dakota, South Dakota, Wyoming, Vermont, and Delaware, all of which have one House member, and the noncitizens of California offset the representation of citizens in the twenty-four states that have five or fewer representatives in the House.

In October 2015, an article cowritten by Paul Goldman (an attorney, journalist, and former chairman of the Democratic Party of Virginia) and Professor Mark J. Rozell (dean of the Schar School of Policy and Government at George Mason University) appeared on Politico.com with the headline: "Illegal Immigrants Could Elect Hillary Clinton." They concluded that "Though they can't cast an actual ballot, [by incorporating noncitizens into electoral college representation] we effectively allow noncitizens to have an indirect, and possibly decisive, say in choosing the President."[7] That is not electoral fraud *per se*, but it underlines the point that elections in the United States are determined by more factors than legal voting.

How we conduct our decennial Census, as well as voter fraud, can decide close races. Yet many local, state, and federal officials are much less worried about stopping fraud that than they are with Census respondents answering whether they are citizens. Their lack of concern is probably not because they don't think voter fraud isn't a problem, but because they think it is a "problem" that benefits their political interests.

As we learned in Chapter One, Democratic Party strategy is strongly tied to outreach to the fast-growing population of Latino immigrants. In criticizing the Trump administration's plan to restore the citizenship question to the Census, Tom Perez, chairman of the Democratic National Committee, even goes so far as to accuse the administration of voter suppression.

"They want to change it to count the number of U.S. citizens so that they can engage in very not subtle voter suppression," Perez said.[8] "This is just another divide-and-conquer effort. This is a first cousin of these voter ID laws sought to make sure that African Americans and Latinos can't vote."

It is remarkable that so many liberals who are outraged by alleged Russian meddling in America's elections—which did not directly manipulate a single vote—are so quick to dismiss demonstrable voter fraud. Even worse, Perez's invocation of the same claims of racism that accompany any effort to secure the country's elections is straight out of the Soros-funded playbook, and only serves to make honest efforts to protect American democracy even more difficult.

The sad fact is that voter fraud in the United States isn't rare, but prosecutions of it are. This is true for several reasons.

First, it takes money and resources to pursue any investigation. Prosecutors just aren't inclined to investigate and bring charges against what, remarkably, are seen to be relatively minor crimes. Secondly, prosecuting voter fraud is incredibly difficult politically, because the Left, as Perez repeatedly demonstrates, tries to smear almost any prosecution of voter fraud as racist, and it takes a brave state attorney general to take that political heat. Local election officials, for their part, celebrate high voter turnout and too often would rather ignore voter fraud than stop it. The good news, J. Christian Adams told me, is that President Trump "is laser-focused on the issue" of voter fraud. "He's educating people, and people are realizing just how big of a problem it is." For the first time in American history we have a president who has made election integrity a priority. It is a priority that all Americans who value democracy and citizens' rights should support. There are several steps local, state, and federal officials could implement to dramatically reduce the threat of modern voter fraud.

As we have shown, there are many different ways that vote fraud can take place. These techniques can be summed up into two groups: fraud by voters, and fraud by political operatives.

The first type, voter fraud, includes various forms of identity theft, lying about one's place of residence or citizenship status, and illegally voting in multiple places. The second type, practiced by political operatives and dishonest or incompetent election officials, includes poor maintenance of voter rolls, obsolete voting equipment, lax absentee ballot policies, and incompetence by election officials.

When we consider the first type, the response of requiring voters to prove they are who they say they are, and are eligible to participate in elections, is obvious. Photo identification is required for so many aspects of life in modern America that requiring it be presented to vote does not seem like too much to ask. Whether it's a driver's license, a passport, or some other state-issued form of ID, with a photo, this step of confirming a voter's identity is practiced in some but certainly not all states. Adopting this policy nationally would go a long way toward deterring attempts by ineligible voters to cast ballots illegally, or to assume the identity of someone else to do so.

Soros-funded groups and the DNC under Tom Perez oppose this idea at every turn, citing the detrimental impact they claim ID requirements have on minority voters. But as we've discussed in the preceding chapters, however, recent elections have shown that even when voter ID laws are implemented, there is no evidence for the charge that they suppress minority turnout.

In early 2017, the *Washington Post* performed a study which it said showed a significant decline in minority participation when voter ID laws were implemented.[9]

But follow-up research raised several questions about the study, which was based on unreliable voter surveys and was also riddled with calculation errors. Analysis by academics from Stanford, Yale, and the University of Pennsylvania showed that when the *Post*'s errors were corrected, there was no statistically significant change in minority voter turnout because of voter ID laws.[10]

A 2017 Alabama Senate race, in fact, saw an increase in minority votes immediately after the state implemented an ID requirement. That race, won by Democratic candidate Doug Jones over the controversial Republican Roy Moore, featured strong get-out-the-vote efforts by Democratic activists. Presenting an ID before voting was clearly no hindrance in that race.

Another commonsense reform would be improved efforts to maintain accurate voting rolls, which, thanks to technology, has never been easier. The problem will always be there to some extent, as Americans die, move, change names, travel, and live in many different places during their lifetimes. The current administration's abortive effort to review systematically the voter rolls of all fifty states may have been too ambitious a first step, but entire industries in the technology field do this kind of "big data" record maintenance every day for commercial customers. Why should the same technology not be applied to something as important as citizens electing their government representatives?

In late May 2018, New Hampshire Secretary of State Bill Gardner and other state officials presented the results of their nearly two-year-long effort to compare the over 94,000 initial double voters they identified through the Interstate Voter Registration Crosscheck Program. Thanks to the Crosscheck program's ability to compare voter data with numerous other states, Gardner and his team were able to narrow down that daunting number to hundreds of actual cases of potential voter fraud.

"That is exactly the kind of thing that I was hoping that the president's integrity commission was going to do at the federal level," Gardner said. "This is valuable."

At the local and state level, officials should make more regular efforts to inspect and verify the accuracy of their voter rolls, which are rife with errors across the country. According to an analysis by the Public Interest Legal Foundation, 148 counties across twenty-four states have voter rolls with more registered voters than legal citizens of a voting age. As PILF's report noted, "recurring impossibly high voter registration rates are the result of a decade or more of negligible list maintenance activities with little to no oversight by state or federal authorities."

The report concluded that "in too many cases, jurisdictions eschew best practices because of limited resources and effort needed to comply with state or federal law."

Best practices should include increased mailings by state and local officials to maintain accurate voter rolls. In Indiana, Secretary of State Connie Lawson sent an address confirmation letter to every registered voter in the state. The process took several years, but concluded with 481,235 registered voters being "properly removed" from Indiana's historically neglected lists of eligible voters.

And then there are the machines that actually count the ballots themselves. Voting systems remain a problem for cash-strapped local jurisdictions. Machines are used past their designed lifespans, poorly secured compared with commercial systems, and cumbersome. Much of their technology is still proprietary, while touchscreen computers are now an everyday item for most people. Instead of continuing to invest in proprietary hardware, why not invest in securable software applications that can be run on a variety of existing computer hardware? Scanner-based systems that use paper ballots are safer than anything else, and give the voter confidence.

Problems related to absentee ballots may be harder to address. People vote absentee for many good reasons, and there's nothing intrinsically wrong with "helping" elderly or ill people to apply and fill in their absentee ballot. Yet it's clear that "helping" often means taking advantage of and misleading vulnerable people, and some political operatives make their careers by doing it, and by delivering absentee ballots by the boxload to elections officials, daring them to object to it. The rules for submitting absentee ballots will never be perfect but enforcing them by matching signatures and other personal identification is reasonable, and in combination with better voter roll maintenance should not be nearly so difficult.

Because GAI did some of the same kind of record-matching that should be standard practice nationwide, we understand that the problem of catching people after the fact will never be easy. It's very expensive and time-consuming to investigate and prosecute someone who may or may not have cast a vote fraudulently. That's why there are so few prosecutions, not because it "never happens," as groups like the Soros-funded Brennan Center and others continue to claim.

This means deterrence, and the adoption of policies that stop fraud from happening in the first place. As with other aspects of our politics today, it won't happen without trust between the two political parties. Just as Republicans have accused Democrats of "condoning voter fraud" because they oppose photo ID laws for voting, Democrats must not declare any effort to make our elections process more secure and accurate as racism and attempts at "voter suppression." Both sides must agree to dial down the rhetoric and address the problems in a straightforward manner that honors that most basic civil right in a democracy—a citizen's right to vote.

Afterword

By Kris Kobach, Secretary of State, State of Kansas

I became interested in voter fraud issues years ago when I saw the left-wing organization "ACORN" committing voter fraud across the country. You might think that a Midwestern state like Kansas wouldn't have the same problems with ballot-stealing, noncitizen voting, or absentee ballot "brokering" that the bigger states and cities run by political machines do.

But, if you know the history of "Bleeding Kansas" right before the Civil War, you know that the Kansas Territory was literally born with pervasive voter fraud, perpetrated by pro-slavery men from Missouri who crossed over the border to vote for slavery-supporting legislators. They fought pitched battles in Kansas with "Free Staters" who sought to bring Kansas into the Union without the stain of slavery.

Eric Eggers's book will be, I hope, a wake-up call to Americans who care about our elections and want them to be fair, honest, and secure. He's documented several patterns across many different states, including fraud through absentee ballots, false statements of citizenship by people registering to vote, and even outright theft of votes. He's done a great service to help stop vote fraud.

It doesn't happen like it did in Bleeding Kansas, at the point of a gun. It happens now at the point of a pen.

Every time a fraudulent vote is cast, it cancels out an honest vote. It's theft of the basic right of American citizens to choose our own leaders and govern ourselves. Politicians who condone it don't deserve to be in office. Political activists who excuse it or hurl charges of "racism" against those who seek to stop it need to take a good, long look at their own part in this crime. They are abetting criminals.

As secretary of state in Kansas, I am our state's chief election official. It's my job to ensure this kind of criminal activity does not take place. I prosecuted multiple cases involving voter fraud, so I can tell you that it happens. I can also tell you that it's sometimes difficult to prosecute these cases. I've learned that it's much more effective to stop voter fraud from happening in the first place than to try to convict someone for having done it. An ounce of prevention is worth a pound of cure.

In Kansas, I authored our law that requires photo identification to vote and proof of citizenship to register. It also provides equivalent security for mail-in ballots. Unfortunately, not enough states have strong laws to keep our elections secure.

So when I was asked by President Trump to help lead the Presidential Commission on Election Integrity, I was happy to help. I have experience, and I know the stakes. We asked each state's chief election official for a copy of their state's publicly available voter information, in order to better investigate voter fraud across the nation. This is the basic information any citizen could walk in off the street and get. The letter went out under my signature.

Immediately, several prominent Democrats declared that they would not comply with this request. California secretary of state Alex Padilla stated, "California's participation would only serve to legitimize the false and already debunked claims of massive voter fraud made by the President, the Vice President, and Mr. Kobach."

Similarly, Virginia's then-Governor Terry McAuliffe fumed, "I have no intention of honoring this request. Virginia conducts fair, honest, and democratic elections, and there is no evidence of significant voter fraud in Virginia."

As you learned from this book, Governor McAuliffe's declaration is particularly amusing, because only three days earlier in Virginia, a college student had been convicted of fraudulently registering eighteen dead people. Evidently, there's plenty of voter fraud in Virginia. Apparently, McAuliffe was ignorant of what's going on in his own state.

Our commission was asked to answer some pretty basic questions. How extensive is voter fraud? How many dead people are registered to vote? How many people are improperly registered? How many people borrowed a page from my own state's past and voted in two (or more) different states in the same election?

In my own state of Kansas, one academic expert has estimated that the number of aliens on the voter rolls may exceed 18,000. In a state like California, that number is likely to be much, much larger. Is that why the California secretary of state didn't want the Commission to look at his state's voter rolls?

For now, we don't know these answers because the commission was prevented from pursuing its research by a barrage of lawsuits from the Left. But, Eric Eggers's book continues the effort to document just how significant voter fraud is. It is important that these facts come to light.

One of the most important ways a state can prevent voter fraud is by requiring proof of citizenship at the time of registration. Only four states—Kansas, Arizona, Georgia, and Alabama—do so.

Requiring voters to have a photo ID is another way. It proves they are who they say they are, and most Americans support it overwhelmingly.

Voting is the most fundamental right of citizenship, and we must treat it with the respect it deserves. It was bought with the blood of patriots, and fraud diminishes the sacrifice they made. We can't let that happen.

My thanks to Eric Eggers for this important work.

Acknowledgments

There may be some people who are able to conceive, research, draft, and edit a book by themselves. I am not one of those people. This book exists only because of the efforts of an entire team with whom I was fortunate enough to work.

At the Government Accountability Institute, we are blessed with some of the brightest and hardest working researchers and staff in the country. Thanks to all of you for your help and support. Special thanks to Caleb Stephens, Christina Armes, Hannah Cooperman, David Brown, and Mark Hoekenga for their help in researching many of the topics this book covers. Thanks also to Tarik Noriega, Steve Post, and Stuart Christmas, who each improved the book in their own way. Joe Duffus provided vital editing, fact checking, and an unyielding advocacy for the removal of any form of the word "impact" as a verb. And this book wouldn't exist without the research and passion of Will Patrick, who discerned and helped develop many of the themes in these pages.

I wouldn't have the chance to work with the incredible team at GAI if I hadn't met Peter Schweizer, whose remarkable talent is exceeded only by his gracious humility. I am deeply indebted to Peter, as well as Wynton Hall for their mentorship and guidance from beginning to end of this process. Thanks also to publicist extraordinaire Sandy Schulz for her advice and help in turning this book into a reality.

Thank you also to the supreme editing talents of Harry Crocker and Nancy Feuerborn, whose work helped refine and sharpen the key points of this book.

Michael Thielen, Jefferson Knight, and J. Christian Adams all have devoted much of their careers to fighting to expose the reality of voter fraud, and took time to educate me on their efforts and experiences.

I'd also like to thank my wife, Dr. Katie Flanagan, for her steadfast support. She was, as she likes to remind me, my first editor when we worked for the Florida State student newspaper, and I continue to benefit from her editorial judgment. Massive thanks also to my young children Elijah, Ashlynne, and Emerson for not destroying Daddy's computer. Good job, guys—you can eat tonight.

In exploring the plight of immigrants who get caught up unsuspectingly into the wide voids of voter registration oversight, immigration attorney Elizabeth Ricci was incredibly helpful and gracious with her time and expertise. Thanks also to David and Joanna Tweedie, who shared their experience as immigrants struggling to navigate the country's confusing laws and guidelines.

Lastly, I have dedicated this book to my grandmother, Fran Thompson, who has worked diligently in her own way to protect the sanctity of American democracy by volunteering as a poll worker in Charleston, South Carolina, for decades' worth of elections.

Appendix

The Number of Double Votes GAI Identified by County in Florida

CITY	COUNT
Orlando	212
Jacksonville	70
Tampa	67
Miami	67
Naples	46
Kissimmee	43
Sarasota	36
Boca Raton	32
Fort Lauderdale	32
Winter Park	27
Port St. Lucie	25
Clearwater	24
Pensacola	24

Fort Myers	24
Boynton Beach	22
Gainesville	22
St. Petersburg	21
Ocala	21
Cape Coral	20
Lake Worth	19
Lakeland	18
West Palm Beach	18
Palm Coast	18
Riverview	17
Winter Garden	17
Melbourne	17
Palm Beach Gardens	16
Pembroke Pines	16
Ormond Beach	16
Tallahassee	16
Port Charlotte	15
The Villages	15
St. Augustine	15
Bonita Springs	15
Hollywood	15

Delray Beach	15
Venice	15
Apopka	15
Plantation	14
Windermere	14
Port Orange	13
Davenport	13
Fort Pierce	13
New Port Richey	13
Bradenton	13
St. Cloud	12
Vero Beach	12
Pompano Beach	12
Miami Beach	11
Fernandina Beach	11
Jupiter	11
Deerfield Beach	11
Brandon	10
Punta Gorda	10
Leesburg	10
Palm Bay	10
Stuart	10

Largo	10
North Port	10
Marco Island	9
Land O' Lakes	9
Orange Park	9
Winter Springs	9
Wesley Chapel	9
Lehigh Acres	9
Altamonte Springs	9
Panama City	9
Spring Hill	9
Sun City Center	9
Titusville	8
Hialeah	8
New Smyrna Beach	8
Wellington	8
Margate	8
Milton	8
Palm Beach	8
Hudson	8
Tamarac	8
Hallandale Beach	8

Daytona Beach	8
Dania Beach	7
Palm Harbor	7
Deland	7
Aventura	7
Homestead	7
Valrico	7
North Fort Myers	7
Parrish	7
Pinellas Park	6
Palmetto	6
Crestview	6
Jacksonville Beach	6
Niceville	6
Maitland	6
Deltona	6
Sanford	6
Oviedo	6
Navarre	6
Clermont	6
Weston	6
Miami Gardens	6

Melbourne Beach	6
Coral Gables	6
Sunrise	5
Lady Lake	5
North Palm Beach	5
Green Cove Springs	5
Wilton Manors	5
Ponte Vedra	5
Haines City	5
Royal Palm Beach	5
Celebration	5
Apollo Beach	5
Cutler Bay	5
Odessa	5
Weeki Wachee	5
Middleburg	5
Gulf Breeze	5
Pinecrest	5
Homosassa	5
Sebastian	5
Dunedin	5
Tarpon Springs	5

Winter Haven	4
Lake Placid	4
Plant City	4
Hobe Sound	4
Sebring	4
Sunny Isle Beach	4
Jensen Beach	4
Brooksville	4
Indialantic	4
Lighthouse Point	4
Lake Mary	4
Mount Dora	4
Inverness	4
North Lauderdale	4
Longwood	4
Moore Haven	4
Wimauma	4
Arcadia	4
Palatka	4
Lutz	4
Barefoot Bay	4
Saint Johns	4

Key Largo	4
Lake Wales	4
Satellite Beach	4
Ponte Vedra Beach	3
Dunnellon	3
Palm City	3
Englewood	3
Highland Beach	3
Riviera Beach	3
Cantonment	3
Davie	3
Atlantic Beach	3
Key West	3
Coral Springs	3
Oldsmar	3
Tyndall Air Force Base	3
Frostproof	3
Miramar	3
Newberry	3
Rockledge	3
Cocoa	3
Seminole	3

Coconut Creek	3
Port Richey	3
Lynn Haven	3
Edgewater	3
Crystal River	3
Lake Alfred	2
Gulfport	2
Lake City	2
Summerfield	2
Southwest Ranches	2
Debary	2
Gulf Stream	2
Ruskin	2
Williston	2
Fort Myers Beach	2
Defuniak Springs	2
Fleming Island	2
Live Oak	2
Yulee	2
Bartow	2
Freeport	2
Tavares	2

Umatilla	2
West Melbourne	2
Crawfordville	2
Bradenton Beach	2
Alva	2
Belle Glade	2
Pace	2
Oakland Park	2
Lauderhill	2
Marathon	2
Juno Beach	2
Merritt Island	2
St. George Island	2
Cape Canaveral	2
Beverly Hills	2
Lake Park	2
Tequesta	2
South Palm Beach	2
Greenacres	2
Mulberry	2
Doral	2
Eastpoint	2

Key West / Key Haven	1
Opa Locka	1
Altoona	1
Lantana	1
Florida City	1
Islamorada /Lower Marathon	1
Lakewood Ranch	1
Treasure Island	1
Sweetwater	1
Santa Rosa Beach	1
Lithia	1
Trinity	1
Fruitland Park	1
Destin	1
Trenton	1
Chipley	1
Fellsmere	1
University Park	1
Nokomis	1
Palm Beach Shores	1
Chiefland	1
Daytona Beach Shores	1

Palm Springs	1
Belleview	1
Temple Terrace	1
Old Town	1
Parkland	1
Panama City Beach	1
Boca Grande	1
Fort McCoy	1
Osprey	1
Tierra Verde	1
McAlpin	1
North Bay Village	1
Gibsonton	1
Starke	1
Fort Meade	1
South Pasadena	1
Baker	1
Redington Shores	1
Miami Springs	1
Quincy	1
Labelle	1
Longboat Key	1

Auburndale	1
Mexico Beach	1
Marianna	1
Crescent City	1
Safety Harbor	1
Lake Butler	1
Paisley	1
Casselberry	1
River Ranch	1
Estero	1
Wildwood	1
Lauderdale-by-the-Sea	1
Valparaiso	1
Gotha	1
Tavernier	1
Hurlburt Field	1
Bay Harbor Islands	1
Sorrento	1
Belleair	1
Okeechobee	1
Miromar Lakes	1
Seffner	1

Cocoa Beach	1
Wauchula	1
Havana	1
Avon Park	1
Pembroke Park	1
West Park	1
Cooper City	1
Citra	1
Minneola	1
St. Pete Beach	1
Big Pine Key	1
Lauderdale Lakes	1
Hastings	1
Ave Maria	1
Indian Harbour Beach	1
Panacea	1
Inglis	1
Madison	1
Polk City	1
North Miami Beach	1
Yalaha	1
Flagler Beach	1

Ochopee	1
Belleair Bluffs	1
St. James City	1
Indian River Shores	1
Clewiston	1
Lee	1
Palmetto Bay	1
Fort Walton Beach	1
Branford	1
Perry	1
Islamorada Park	1
Groveland	1
Bronson	1
North Venice	1
Dover	1
Key Biscayne	1
Hypoluxo	1
Chattahoochee	1
TOTAL	**2166**

Notes

Introduction

1. "Myth of Voter Fraud," Brennan Center for Justice, accessed April 12, 2018, https://www.brennancenter.org/issues/voter-fraud.
2. Lawrence Mower, "Exclusive: Voter Fraud in Palm Beach County: State Attorney Finds Crimes, but No Suspect," *Palm Beach Post*, July 23, 2017, https://www.mypalmbeachpost.com/news/exclusive-voter-fraud-palm-beach-county-state-attorney-finds-crimes-but-suspect/buShkHum7thKuTKE8F69QO/.
3. Justin Levitt, *The Truth about Voter Fraud*, Brennan Center for Justice, accessed April 12, 2018, https://www.brennancenter.org/sites/default/files/legacy/The%20Truth%20About%20Voter%20Fraud.pdf.
4. Adam Liptak, "Error and Fraud at Issue as Absentee Voting Rises," *New York Times*, October 6, 2012, http://www.nytimes.com/2012/10/07/us/politics/as-more-vote-by-mail-faulty-ballots-could-impact-elections.html.

5. Sam Levine, "Another State Shows Voter Fraud Isn't a Widespread Problem," Huffington Post, April 21, 2017, https://www.huffingtonpost.com/entry/north-carolina-voter-fraud_us_58fa5b2fe4b06b9cb916ba6c.

6. "Garden State Gotcha," Public Interest Legal Foundation, September 2017, https://publicinterestlegal.org/files/Garden-State-Gotcha_PILF.pdf.

7. David Gelles, "George Soros Transfers Billions to Open Society Foundations," *New York Times*, October 17, 2017, https://www.nytimes.com/2017/10/17/business/george-soros-open-society-foundations.html.

8. "Introduction of the Streamlined and Improved Methods at Polling Locations and Early Voting Act," Congressional Record, 115th Congress, 1st Session, Issue: Vol. 163, No. 17—Daily Edition, February 1, 2017, https://www.congress.gov/congressional-record/2017/2/1/extensions-of-remarks-section/article/e118-3?q=%7B%22search%22%3A%5B%22voter+id%22%5D%7D&r=6&overview=open#content.

9. "S.1547 – Anti-Voter Suppression Act," Congress.gov, accessed April 12, 2018, https://www.congress.gov/bill/115th-congress/senate-bill/1547/text.

10. Bill Barrow, Marc Levy, and Steve Peoples, "PA Race Razor Close; Dem Lamb Claims Win, GOP Not Conceding," Associated Press, March 14, 2018, https://apnews.com/cfd30a7393a444578703ca8af7bb6dc4.

Chapter 1 The Future Is Now—Tom Perez

1. Donna Brazile, "Inside Hillary Clinton's Secret Takeover of the DNC," Politico Magazine, November 2, 2017, https://www.politico.com/magazine/story/2017/11/02/clinton-brazile-hacks-2016-215774.

2. Jonathan Martin, "Democrats Elect Thomas Perez, Establishment Favorite, as Party Chairman," *New York Times*, February 25, 2017, https://www.nytimes.com/2017/02/25/us/politics/dnc-perez-ellison-chairman-election.html.

3. Ibid.

4. "Meet Tom," Team Tom website, accessed April 12, 2018, https:// www.tomperez.org/meet-tom/.

5. "U.S. Programs: Casa De Maryland Inc.," Open Society Foundations, accessed April 12, 2018, https://www.opensocietyfoundations.org/ about/programs/us-programs/grantees/casa-de-maryland-inc-1.

6. John Fund, "Meet the DNC's New Organizer in Chief," *National Review*, February 26, 2017, http://www.nationalreview.com/ article/445257/tom-perez-dnc-chief-hardcore-progressive.

7. Internet Archive: Way Back Machine, accessed April 12, 2018, https:// web.archive.org/web/20070708073133/http://www.dclabor.org/ht/a/ GetDocumentAction/i/10665.

8. Andrew A. Green, "Perez Enters Race for Attorney General," *Baltimore Sun*, May 24, 2006, http://articles.baltimoresun.com/2006-05-24/news/0605240230_1_attorney-general-montgomery-county-candidacy.

9. Jerry Markon and Krissah Thompson, "Dispute over New Black Panthers Case Causes Deep Divisions," *Washington Post*, October 22, 2010, http://www.washingtonpost.com/wp-dyn/content/ article/2010/10/22/AR2010102203982.html.

10. U.S. Department of Justice, Office of the Inspector General, Oversight and Review Division, *A Review of the Operations of the Voting Section of the Civil Rights Division*, March 2013, https://oig.justice. gov/reports/2013/s1303.pdf.

11. Esther Yu Hsi Lee, "Non-Citizens Now Allowed to Vote in Maryland City's Local Elections," ThinkProgress, September 13, 2017, https:// thinkprogress.org/college-park-md-local-elections-ffc7accd7ab0/.

12. Maggie Astor, "Maryland City May Let Noncitizens Vote, a Proposal with Precedent," *New York Times*, August 9, 2017, https://www. nytimes.com/2017/08/09/us/college-park-immigrant-voting-rights. html.

13. Brooke Singman, "'Slippery Slope'? Cities across the Country Allowing Non-Citizens to Vote," Fox News Politics, September 15, 2017, http://www.foxnews.com/politics/2017/09/15/slippery-slope-cities-across-country-allowing-non-citizens-to-vote.html.

14. Spencer S. Hsu, "Measure to Let Noncitizens Vote Actually Failed, College Park Announces," *Washington Post*, September 16, 2017,

https://www.washingtonpost.com/local/md-politics/measure-to-let-noncitizens-vote-actually-failed-college-park-md-announces-with-considerable-embarrassment/2017/09/16/2f973582-9ae9-11e7-b569-3360011663b4_story.html?utm_term=.5a2e2870fa97.

15. Aaron Kraut, "Takoma Park Stands by Non-U.S. Citizen Voting Law," *Washington Post*, March 14, 2012, https://www.washingtonpost.com/local/takoma-park-stands-by-non-us-citizen-voting-law/2012/03/13/gIQAVBcgBS_story.html?utm_term=.8eaa97b2e844.

16. "Updated: Democrats Pick Tom Perez to Head DC (Video)," Montgomery Community Media, February 26, 2017, http://www.mymcmedia.org/democrats-pick-tom-perez-to-head-dnc/.

17. Edward-Isaac Dovere, "DNC Overhaul Struggles as Sanders-Clinton Rivalries Persist," Politico, January 16, 2018, https://www.politico.com/story/2018/01/16/democrats-clinton-sanders-reforms-340616.

18. Amie Parnes, "Obama Plays Behind-the-Scenes Role in Rebuilding Democratic Party," *Hill*, July 2, 2017, http://thehill.com/homenews/campaign/340314-obama-plays-behind-the-scenes-role-in-rebuilding-democratic-party.

19. Amie Parnes and Jonathan Easley, "Obama Fingerprints at DNC?" *Hill*, April 11, 2017, http://thehill.com/homenews/campaign/328338-obama-fingerprints-at-dnc.

20. Mark Hugo Lopez, "The Hispanic Vote in the 2008 Election," Pew Research Center, November 5, 2008, updated November 7, 2008, http://www.pewhispanic.org/2008/11/05/the-hispanic-vote-in-the-2008-election/.

21. Mark Hugo Lopez and Paul Taylor, "Latino Voters in the 2012 Election," Pew Research Center, November 7, 2012, http://www.pewhispanic.org/2012/11/07/latino-voters-in-the-2012-election/.

22. Jens Manuel Krogstad and Mark Hugo Lopez, "Black Voter Turnout Fell in 2016, Even as a Record Number of Americans Cast Ballots," Pew Research Center, May 12, 2017, http://www.pewresearch.org/fact-tank/2017/05/12/black-voter-turnout-fell-in-2016-even-as-a-record-number-of-americans-cast-ballots/.

23. Jens Manuel Krogstad and Mark Hugo Lopez, "Hillary Clinton Won Latino Vote but Fell below 2012 Support for Obama," Pew Research Center, November 29, 2016, http://www.pewresearch.org/fact-tank/2016/11/29/hillary-clinton-wins-latino-vote-but-falls-below-2012-support-for-obama/.

24. Lopez and Taylor, "Latino Voters in the 2012 Election."

25. Stephen A. Nuno, "Opinion: Democrats Must Go Left if They Want More Latino Voters," NBC News, February 24, 2017, https://www.nbcnews.com/news/latino/opinion-democrats-must-go-left-if-they-want-more-latino-n724316.

26. Manuel Pastor, "Latinos and the Future of American Politics," American Prospect, January 17, 2017, http://prospect.org/article/latinos-and-future-american-politics.

27. Susan Milligan, "Return of the Rising American Electorate," *U.S. News & World Report,* December 1, 2017, https://www.usnews.com/news/the-report/articles/2017-12-01/democrats-must-focus-on-minorities-women-and-white-men-to-win.

28. Musa al-Gharbi, "The Democratic Party Is Facing a Demographic Crisis," Huffington Post, March 1, 2017, updated March 1, 2017, https://www.huffingtonpost.com/entry/the-democratic-party-is-facing-a-demographic-crisis_us_58b6d16ce4b0658fc20f9c0c.

29. Mark Hugo Lopez, Ana Gonzalez-Barrera, Jens Manuel Krogstad, and Gustavo López, "4. Latinos and the Political Parties," Pew Research Center, October 11, 2016, http://www.pewhispanic.org/2016/10/11/latinos-and-the-political-parties/.

30. Antonio Flores, "How the U.S. Hispanic Population Is Changing," Pew Research Center, September 18, 2017, http://www.pewresearch.org/fact-tank/2017/09/18/how-the-u-s-hispanic-population-is-changing/.

31. "Two-Thirds of Hispanic Voters Identify with or Lean toward the Democratic Party," Pew Research Center, October 10, 2016, http://www.pewhispanic.org/2016/10/11/democrats-maintain-edge-as-party-more-concerned-for-latinos-but-views-similar-to-2012/ph_2016-10-11_politics_4-02/.

32. Flores, "Hispanic Population Is Changing."

33. "Mark Steyn: How the GOP: Earned Its Date with Destiny," *Orange County Register*, November 16, 2012, https://www.ocregister.com/2012/11/16/mark-steyn-how-the-gop-earned-its-date-with-destiny/.

34. "U.S. Hispanic Population Hits New High," Pew Research Center, September 18, 2017, http://www.pewresearch.org/fact-tank/2017/09/18/how-the-u-s-hispanic-population-is-changing/ft_17-09-18_hispanics_ushispanicpop/.

35. Jeffrey S. Passel and D'Vera Cohn, "As Mexican Share Declined, U.S. Unauthorized Immigrant Population Fell in 2015 below Recession Level," Pew Research Center, April 25, 2017, http://www.pewresearch.org/fact-tank/2017/04/25/as-mexican-share-declined-u-s-unauthorized-immigrant-population-fell-in-2015-below-recession-level/.

36. Philip Bump, "Donald Trump Will Be President Thanks to 80,000 People in Three States," *Washington Post*, December 1, 2016, https://www.washingtonpost.com/news/the-fix/wp/2016/12/01/donald-trump-will-be-president-thanks-to-80000-people-in-three-states/?utm_term=.d79de1f6ff9e.

37. Rachel Chason, "Non-Citizens Can Now Vote in Colleg Park, Md.," *Washington Post*, September 13, 2017, https://www.washingtonpost.com/local/md-politics/college-park-decides-to-allow-noncitizens-to-vote-in-local-elections/2017/09/13/2b7adb4a-987b-11e7-87fc-c3f7ee4035c9_story.html?utm_term=.ced6c802146c.

38. "Noncitizens Will Soon Be Able to Vote in San Francisco—for School Board," National Public Radio, heard on *All Things Considered*, May 3, 2017, https://www.npr.org/2017/05/03/526703128/non-citizens-will-soon-be-able-to-vote-in-san-francisco-for-school-board.

39. Carl Campanile, "New Bill Could Give Illegal Aliens Voting Rights in New York City," *New York Post*, February 22, 2016, https://nypost.com/2016/02/22/new-bill-could-give-illegal-aliens-voting-rights-in-new-york-city/.

40. Liz Robbins, "New York Can Destroy Documents, Judge Rules in Municipal ID Case," *New York Times*, April 2, 2017, https://www.nytimes.com/2017/04/07/nyregion/new-york-can-destroy-documents-judge-rules-in-municipal-id-case.html?mtrref=www.google.com.

41. Ibid.

42. John Byrne, "Emanuel Unveils New Municipal ID, but Public Can't Get Them until March," *Chicago Tribune*, December 14, 2017, http://www.chicagotribune.com/news/local/politics/ct-met-rahm-emanuel-municipal-id-launch-20171214-story.html.

43. 18 USC 611: Voting by Aliens, text contains those laws in effect on April 15, 2018, accessed April 16, 2018, http://uscode.house.gov/view.xhtml?req=(title:18%20section:611%20edition:prelim)%20OR%20(granuleid:USC-prelim-title18-section611)&f=treesort&edition=prelim&num=0&jumpTo=true.

44. Dara Lind, "The Disastrous, Forgotten 1996 Law That Created Today's Immigration Problem," Vox, April 28, 2016, https://www.vox.com/2016/4/28/11515132/iirira-clinton-immigration.

45. Mr. Grijalva, Resolution, 114th Congress, 2d Session, April 21, 2016, https://grijalva.house.gov/uploads/GRIJAL_098_xml.pdf.

46. "Most Democrats Think Illegal Immigrants Should Vote," Rasmussen Reports, May 29, 2015, http://www.rasmussenreports.com/public_content/politics/general_politics/may_2015/most_democrats_think_illegal_immigrants_should_vote.

47. Tom Perez and Karen Carter Peterson, "DNC Chairman: The Democratic Plan to Combat Trump's Voter Suppression Commission," *Time*, July 19, 2017, http://time.com/4864109/dnc-trump-voter-fraud-election-commission/.

48. Cheryl K. Chumley, "Eric Holder: 'I Will Proudly Accept That Label' of Activist Attorney General," *Washington Times*, August 4, 2014, https://www.washingtontimes.com/news/2014/aug/4/eric-holder-i-will-proudly-accept-label-activist-a/.

49. "Supreme Court Strikes Down Key Provision of Voting Rights Law," National Public Radio, June 25, 2013, https://www.npr.org/sections/thetwo-way/2013/06/25/195506795/supreme-court-strikes-down-key-provision-of-voting-rights-law.

50. Sean Sullivan and Sari Horwitz, "Federal Appeals Court Rules against Ohio Voter-Roll Purges," *Washington Post*, September 23, 2016, https://www.washingtonpost.com/politics/federal-appeals-court-rules-against-ohio-voter-roll-purges/2016/09/23/67c1311e-81b4-11e6-a52d-9a865a0ed0d4_story.html?utm_term=.8fa1bb248149.

51. Sari Horwitz, "Justice Department Changes Its Position in High-Profile Texas Voter-ID Case," *Washington Post*, February 27, 2017, https://www.washingtonpost.com/world/national-security/justice-department-changes-its-position-in-high-profile-texas-voter-id-case/2017/02/27/cfaafac0-fd0c-11e6-99b4-9e613afeb09f_story.html?utm_term=.215ef712083e.

52. Jane C. Timm, "Justice Department Reverses Position in Ohio Voting Rights Case," NBC News, August 8, 2017, updated August 8, 2017, https://www.nbcnews.com/politics/supreme-court/justice-department-reverses-position-ohio-voting-rights-case-n790846.

53. Justin Levitt, "The Truth about Voter Fraud," Brennan Center for Justice, November 9, 2007, https://www.brennancenter.org/publication/truth-about-voter-fraud.

54. "Presidential Advisory Commission on Election Integrity," WhiteHouse.gov, July 13, 2017, https://www.whitehouse.gov/articles/presidential-advisory-commission-election-integrity/.

55. "Legal Actions Taken against Trump's 'Voter Fraud' Commission," Brennan Center for Justice, updated December 26, 2017, https://www.brennancenter.org/legal-actions-taken-against-trump%E2%80%99s-%E2%80%9Cfraud%E2%80%9D-commission.

56. Robert Knight, "A Hard Look at a Holder Holdover," *Washington Times*, December 3, 2017, https://www.washingtontimes.com/news/2017/dec/3/why-the-justice-department-is-ignoring-widespread-/.

Chapter 2 George Soros—the Man behind the Ballot Booth

1. Justin McCarthy, "Four in Five Americans Support Voter ID Laws, Early Voting," Gallup, August 22, 2016, http://news.gallup.com/poll/194741/four-five-americans-support-voter-laws-early-voting.aspx.

2. Ibid.

3. Mario Trujillo, "Poll: 70 Percent Support Voter ID Laws," *Hill*, May 15, 2014, http://thehill.com/blogs/blog-briefing-room/206300-poll-70-percent-support-voter-id-laws.

4. Michael Brandon and Jon Cohen, "Poll: Concerns about Voter Fraud Spur Broad Support for Voter ID Laws," *Washington Post*, August

11, 2012, https://www.washingtonpost.com/politics/poll-concerns-about-voter-fraud-spur-broad-support-for-voter-id-laws/2012/08/11/40db3aba-e2fb-11e1-ae7f-d2a13e249eb2_story.html?utm_term=.28f8c1ef7c21.

5. Shannon McCaffrey, "Despite Voter ID Law, Minority Turnout up in Georgia," *Atlanta Journal-Constitution,* September 3, 2012, http://www.ajc.com/news/despite-voter-law-minority-turnout-georgia/3wOfD2SkXmTgRwbySd2ZiK/.

6. Shannon McCaffrey, "Despite Voter ID Law, Minority Turnout up in Georgia," *Atlanta Journal-Constitution,* September 3, 2012, http://www.ajc.com/news/despite-voter-law-minority-turnout-georgia/3wOfD2SkXmTgRwbySd2ZiK/.

7. Alan Blinder and Michael Wines, "Black Turnout in Alabama Complicates Debate on Voting Laws," *New York Times,* December 24, 2017, https://www.nytimes.com/2017/12/24/us/alabama-voting-blacks-.html.

8. "Does a BEAR Leak in the Woods?," ThreatConnect, August 12, 2016, https://www.threatconnect.com/blog/does-a-bear-leak-in-the-woods/.

9. "The Bizarre Media Blackout of Hacked George Soros Documents," *Investor's Business Daily,* August 19, 2016, https://www.investors.com/politics/editorials/the-bizarre-media-blackout-of-hacked-george-soros-documents/.

10. Constitution and the Courts Portfolio Review, May 21, 2015, https://webcache.googleusercontent.com/search?q=cache:o1SJEKqei1AJ:https://fdik.org/soros.dcleaks.com/download/index.html%253Ff%3D%25252F2015%252520materials%252520from%252520staff%252520level%252520portfolio%252520reviews%252520documents%252520for%252520internal%252520use%252520only%25252Fus%252520programs%252520usp%252520democracy%252520fund%252520constitution%252520and%252520the%252520courts%252520may%25252021%2525202015%25252Fusp%252520dem%252520fund%252520+&cd=1&hl=en&ct=clnk&gl=us&client=opera.

11. "Grantees," Open Society Foundations, accessed April 17, 2018, https://www.opensocietyfoundations.org/about/programs/ us-programs/grantees.

12. David Gelles, "George Soros Transfers Billions to Open Society Foundations," *New York Times*, October 17, 2017, https://www. nytimes.com/2017/10/17/business/george-soros-open-society-foundations.html.

13. Ibid.

14. Examiner Staff Writer, "The Sleazy Tactics of George Soros," *Washington Examiner*, September 10, 2007, http://www. washingtonexaminer.com/the-sleazy-tactics-of-george-soros/ article/83924.

15. "The Life of George Soros," GeorgeSoros.com, accessed April 17, 2018, https://www.georgesoros.com/the-life-of-george-soros/.

16. "Staff: George Soros," Open Society Foundations, accessed April 17, 2018, https://www.opensocietyfoundations.org/people/george-soros.

17. "Insider Trading Conviction of Soros Is Upheld," *New York Times*, June 14, 2006, http://www.nytimes.com/2006/06/14/business/ worldbusiness/14iht-soros.1974397.html.

18. Stefan Kanfer, "Connoisseur of Chaos: The Dystopian Visions of George Soros, Billionaire Funder of the Left," *City Journal*, Winter 2017, https://www.city-journal.org/html/connoisseur-chaos-14954. html.

19. Paul Krugman, *The Accidental Theorist: And Other Dispatches from the Dismal Science*, https://books.google.com/books?id=DNRS1rbO 5IQC&pg=PA160&lpg=PA160&dq=The+accidental+theorist:+and+ other+dispatches+from+the+dismal+science+soroi&source=bl&ots= u5P7PRtRMS&sig=qhQzzrrCKLkx_NmHWEbXRqYdh0E&hl=en &sa=X&ved=0ahUKEwii856RpavZAhWHq1MKHcHGBl0Q6AEI RjAE#v=onepage&q=soroi&f=false.

20. Christian Datoc, "George Soros' 'Open Society Foundations' Named 2016's LEAST Transparent Think Tank," Daily Caller, July 6, 2016, http://dailycaller.com/2016/07/06/george-soros-open-society-foundations-named-2016s-least-transparent-think-tank/.

21. Sirena Bergman, "Who Is George Soros? What You Need to Know about the Man Who 'Broke the Bank of England' and Now Wants to

Stop Brexit," Metro, February 8, 2018, http://metro.co.uk/2018/02/08/who-is-george-soros-what-you-need-to-know-about-the-man-who-broke-the-bank-of-england-and-now-wants-to-stop-brexit-7296523/.

22. Scott Johnson, "A Gun Smokes in Minnesota," Powerline blog, October 28, 2004, http://www.powerlineblog.com/archives/2004/10/008279.php.

23. Chuck Neubauer, "Soros and Liberal Groups Seeking Top Election Posts in Battleground States," *Washington Times*, June 23, 2011, https://www.washingtontimes.com/news/2011/jun/23/section-527-works-to-seat-liberals-as-election-ove/.

24. Robert Barnes, "The Crusade of a Democratic Superlawyer with Multimillion-Dollar Backing," *Washington Post*, August 7, 2016, https://www.washingtonpost.com/politics/courts_law/the-crusade-of-a-democratic-super-lawyer-with-multimillion-dollar-backing/2016/08/07/2c1b408c-5a54-11e6-9767-f6c947fd0cb8_story.html.

25. Ibid.

26. Ibid.

27. Adam Entous, Devlin Barrett, and Rosalind S. Helderman, "Clinton Campaign, DNC Paid for Research That Led to Russia Dossier," *Washington Post*, October 24, 2017, https://www.washingtonpost.com/world/national-security/clinton-campaign-dnc-paid-for-research-that-led-to-russia-dossier/2017/10/24/226fabf0-b8e4-11e7-a908-a3470754bbb9_story.html?utm_term=.05b1e7bd0bde.

28. Joe Schoffstall, "Clinton Lawyers, Soros Back Anti-Voter ID Lawsuits," Washington Free Beacon, June 26, 2015, http://freebeacon.com/politics/clinton-lawyer-soros-back-anti-voter-id-lawsuits/.

29. Cliff Pinckard, "Ohio Woman Sent to Jail for False Voter Registrations, Including Dead People," Metro News, March 7, 2017, updated March 7, 2017, http://www.cleveland.com/metro/index.ssf/2017/03/ohio_woman_sent_to_jail_for_fa.html.

30. "Virginia Democrats to Appeal Voter ID Case," *Daily Press*, May 26, 2016, http://www.dailypress.com/news/politics/dp-nws-voter-id-appeal-20160526-story.html.

31. "One Third of Noncitizens Found Voted Illegally," Public Interest Legal Foundation, May 29, 2017, https://publicinterestlegal.org/blog/report-5500-noncitizens-discovered-voter-rolls-virginia/.

32. DCLeaks Soros docs.

33. NAACP LDF website, Our Staff, http://www.naacpldf.org/staff.

34. Rachel Weiner, "Federal Court Rejects Challenge to Trump Voting Commission," *Washington Post*, December 26, 2017, https://www.washingtonpost.com/local/public-safety/federal-court-rejects-challenge-to-trump-voter-commission/2017/12/26/f1f64f42-ea61-11e7-9f92-10a2203f6c8d_story.html?noredirect=on.

35. Government Accountability Institute, America the Vulnerable: The Problem of Duplicate Voting, http://g-a-i.org/wp-content/uploads/2017/07/Voter-Fraud-Final-with-Appendix-1.pdf.

36. "Soros Spends over $48 Million Funding Media Organizations," Media Research Center, accessed April 17, 2018, https://www.mrc.org/commentary/soros-spends-over-48-million-funding-media-organizations.

37. "Testimony of Catherine Engelbrecht," February 6, 2014, https://oversight.house.gov/wp-content/uploads/2014/02/Engelbrecht.pdf.

38. "About Us," True the Vote, accessed April 17, 2018, https://truethevote.org/aboutus.

39. Ibid.

40. "About Us," The Campaign Legal Center, accessed December 7, 2017, https://web.archive.org/web/20171207070036/http://www.campaignlegalcenter.org/about/funding.

41. "The Campaign Legal Center," Ballotpedia, accessed May 21, 2018, https://ballotpedia.org/The_Campaign_Legal_Center.

42. Sen. Ted Cruz, "Catherine Engelbrecht's Testimony at House of Representatives Hearing on IRS Targeting," YouTube, February 6, 2014, https://www.youtube.com/watch?v=xxcMKtsm5BU.

43. "Testimony of Catherine Engelbrecht."

44. Ibid.

45. "Rep. Cummings Launches Investigation of "True the Vote"; Raises Questions about Conservative Group's Campaign to Challenge Legitimate Voters," United States Congressman Elijah E. Cummings, October 5, 2012, https://cummings.house.gov/press-release/

cummings-launches-investigation-%E2%80%9Ctrue-vote%E2%80%9D-raises-questions-about-conservative-group.

46. "The IRS Targeting Investigation: What Is the Administration Doing?" Oversight & Government Reform, Hearding Date: February 6, 2014, https://oversight.house.gov/hearing/irs-targeting-investigation-administration/.

47. "Cummings Launches Investigation of 'True the Vote'; Raises Questions about Conservative Group's Campaign to Challenge Legitimate Voters," House Committee on Oversight website, October 5, 2012, https://democrats-oversight.house.gov/news/press-releases/cummings-launches-investigation-of-true-the-vote-raises-questions-about.

48. Hans von Spakovsky, "Rep. Elijah Cummings (D-MD) Threatans Citizens Group over Election Integrity," Daily Signal, October 11, 2012, http://dailysignal.com/2012/10/11/rep-elijah-cummings-d-md-threatens-citizens-group-over-election-integrity/.

49. Peter Overby, "IRS Apologizes for Aggressive Scrutiny of Conservative Groups," National Public Radio, October 27, 2017, https://www.npr.org/2017/10/27/560308997/irs-apologizes-for-aggressive-scrutiny-of-conservative-groups.

50. Catherine Engelbrecht, "True the Vote v. IRS Consent Order," Scribd, Inc., January 21, 2018, https://www.scribd.com/document/369806983/True-the-Vote-v-IRS-Consent-Order-Jan-21-2018#from_embed.

51. "Testimony of Catherine Engelbrecht."

52. DCLeaks Soros docs.

53. Complaint for Declaratory and Injunctive Relief, https://ag.ny.gov/sites/default/files/complaint.pdf.

Chapter 3 We've Been Here Before: A Brief History of Voter Fraud

1. Paul Bedard, "George Washington Plied Voters with Booze," *U.S. News & World Report*, November 8, 2011, https://www.usnews.com/news/blogs/washington-whispers/2011/11/08/george-washington-plied-voters-with-booze.

2. John G. Kolp, "Elections in Colonial Virginia," Encyclopedia Virginia, accessed April 17, 2018, https://www.encyclopediavirginia.org/Elections_in_Colonial_Virginia .

3. Tracy Campbell, *Deliver the Vote* (New York: Carroll & Graf Publishers, 2005), 5.

4. Campbell, *Deliver the Vote*, 7–8.

5. "Who Voted in Early America?," Constitutional Rights Foundation, accessed April 17, 2018, http://www.crf-usa.org/bill-of-rights-in-action/bria-8-1-b-who-voted-in-early-america.

6. Tom Huskerson, "A Brief History of Voter Registration in the United States," Independent Voter Network, September 8, 2014, https://ivn.us/2014/09/08/brief-history-voter-registration-united-states/.

7. http://archives.lib.state.ma.us/actsResolves/1800/1800acts0074.pdf ; Lily Rothman, "For National Voter Registration Day, Here's How Registering to Vote Became a Thing," *Time*, September 26, 2016, http://time.com/4502154/voter-registration-history/.

8. Daniel P. Tokaji, "Voter Registration and Election Reform," *William & Mary Bill of Rights Journal*, volume 17, issue 2, article 3, http://scholarship.law.wm.edu/cgi/viewcontent.cgi?article=1027&context=wmborj.

9. Campbell, *Deliver the Vote*, 15.

10. Joseph P. Harris, *Registration of Voters in the United States* (Washington: The Brookings Institution, 1929), https://babel.hathitrust.org/cgi/pt?id=uc1.$b22360;view=1up;seq=89;size=75, 67.

11. *See* S. J. Ackerman, "The Vote That Failed," Smithsonian.com, November 1998, https://www.smithsonianmag.com/history/the-vote-that-failed-159427766/#Xmf2KDqhufjCr0uy.99.

12. Natalie Zarrelli, "Election Fraud in the 1800s Involved Kidnapping and Forced Drinking," Atlas Obscura, September 7, 2016, https://www.atlasobscura.com/articles/election-fraud-in-the-1800s-involved-kidnapping-and-forced-drinking.

13. Michael E. Woods, "Fraud, Violence, and 'Rigged' Elections: A Warning from Bleeding Kansas," Journal of the Civil War Era, September 6, 2016, https://journalofthecivilwarera.org/2016/09/fraud-violence-rigged-elections-warning-bleeding-kansas/.

14. Kevin Olson, Kevin, *Frontier Manhattan: Yankee Settlement to Kansas Town, 1854–1894* (University Press of Kansas).

15. Barbara Finlay, "Voter Fraud in the Real World," HistoryNet, October 3, 2016, http://www.historynet.com/voter-fraud.htm.

16. John Fund, "How to Steal and Election," CJ, Autumn 2004, https://
     www.city-journal.org/html/how-steal-election-12824.html.
17. Ibid.
18. Ibid.
19. "A Brief History of Election 'Rigging' in the United States," History
     Extra, November 3, 2016, http://www.historyextra.com/period/
     modern/a-brief-history-of-election-rigging-in-the-united-states/.
20. David Iaconangelo, "When American Elections Were Rigged: How
     Did the US Stop Electoral Fraud?," *Christian Science Monitor*,
     October 21, 2016, https://www.csmonitor.com/USA/
     Politics/2016/1021/When-American-elections-were-rigged-How-did-
     the-US-stop-electoral-fraud.
21. "Secret Ballot," Wikipedia, accessed April 17, 2018, https://
     en.wikipedia.org/wiki/Secret_ballot.
22. Campbell, *Deliver the Vote*, 131.
23. Tracy A. Campbell, "Machine Politics, Police Corruption, and the
     Persistence of Vote Fraud: The Case of the Louisville, Kentucky,
     Election of 1905," Journal of Policy History, Volume 15, Issue 3, July
     2003, pp. 269–300, https://www.cambridge.org/core/journals/
     journal-of-policy-history/article/machine-politics-police-corruption-
     and-the-persistence-of-vote-fraud-the-case-of-the-louisville-kentucky-
     election-of-1905/AEBC5068E269F5A98568A0A16C5B68D7.
24. file:///C:/Users/steve.stewart/Downloads/Campbell%20-%20
     2003%20-%20Machine%20Politics,%20Police%20Corruption,%20
     and%20the%20Persi.pdf.
25. Fund, "How to Steal an Election."
26. "A Brief History of Election 'Rigging' in the United States," History
     Extra, November 3, 2016, http://www.historyextra.com/period/
     modern/a-brief-history-of-election-rigging-in-the-united-states/ .
27. "The Misleading Myth of Voter Fraud in American Elections,"
     Scholars Strategy Network, January 28, 2014, https://scholars.org/
     brief/misleading-myth-voter-fraud-american-elections.
28. Alissa J. Rubin and Aaron Zitner, "Vote Fraud a Tradition in Political
     Yesteryear," *Los Angeles Times*, November 9, 2000, http://articles.
     latimes.com/2000/nov/09/news/mn-49508.

29. Michael deCourcy Hinds, "Vote-Fraud Ruling Shifts Pennsylvania Senate," *New York Times*, 1994, http://www.nytimes.com/1994/02/19/us/vote-fraud-ruling-shifts-pennsylvania-senate.html.
30. Source: Book proposal.

Chapter 4 The American Dream—The Problem with Noncitizen Voting

1. "Non-Citizens Registered to Vote in Lawrence, but Officials Shrug," Boston 25 News, November 5, 2012, http://www.fox25boston.com/news/noncitizens-registered-to-vote-in-lawrence-but-officials-shrug-1/139165724.
2. Ibid.
3. Ibid.
4. "NBC2 Investigates: Voter Fraud," NBC2, February 2, 2012, updated February 2, 2012, http://www.nbc-2.com/story/16662854/2012/02/Thursday/nbc2-investigates-voter-fraud.
5. Ibid.
6. Ibid.
7. Ibid.
8. "Why Don't We Verify Voter Citizenship?," *Las Vegas Review-Journal*, November 11, 2012, https://www.reviewjournal.com/opinion/why-dont-we-verify-voter-citizenship/ .
9. "How Many NonCitizens Are Registered to Vote?," *Las Vegas Review-Journal*, November 4, 2012, https://www.reviewjournal.com/opinion/how-many-noncitizens-are-registered-to-vote/.
10. Elizabeth Crum, "Harrah's Bosses Put Squeeze on Employees to Vote in Pro-Reid Effort," *National Review*, November 2, 2010, https://www.nationalreview.com/2010/11/harrahs-bosses-put-squeeze-employees-vote-pro-reid-effort-elizabeth-crum/.
11. "In Photos: The Damning Email Chain Showing Harrah's Execs Colluding with Harry Reid's Campaign, Forcing Their Employees to Vote Democrat," Doug Ross @ Journal, November 3, 2010, http://directorblue.blogspot.com/2010/11/in-photos-damning-email-chain-from.html.

12. "How Many Noncitizens Are Registered to Vote?," *Las Vegas Review-Journal*, November 4, 2012, https://www.reviewjournal.com/opinion/how-many-noncitizens-are-registered-to-vote.
13. Ibid.
14. Michael Wines, "A Texas Woman 'Voted like a U.S. Citizen.' Only She Wasn't.," *New York Times*, March 18, 2017, https://www.nytimes.com/2017/03/18/us/voter-fraud-fort-worth-trial-rosa-marie-ortega.html.
15. Ibid.
16. Mitch Mitchell, "Grand Prairie Woman Accused of Voter Fraud Goes on Trial," *Star-Telegram*, February 7, 2017, updated February 7, 2017, http://www.star-telegram.com/news/local/community/fort-worth/article131365129.html.
17. Wines, "Texas Woman 'Voted like a U.S. Citizen.'"
18. Wines, Michael, Illegal Voting Gets Texas Woman 8 Years in Prison, and Certain Deportation," *New York Times*, February 10, 2017, https://www.nytimes.com/2017/02/10/us/illegal-voting-gets-texas-woman-8-years-in-prison-and-certain-deportation.html.
19. Ibid.
20. Mitch Mitchell, "In a Case That 'Sends a Message,' Mom Gets Eight Years in Prison for Voting Illegally," *Star-Telegram*, February 9, 2017, http://www.star-telegram.com/news/local/community/fort-worth/article131719624.html/
21. James Ragland, "Rosa Maria Ortega Is Free on Bond, and, for Now, the System's Done the Right Thing," Dallas News, March 2017, https://www.dallasnews.com/opinion/commentary/2017/03/03/rosa-maria-ortega-free-bond-now-systems-done-right-thing.
22. Mitch Mitchell, "Grand Prairie Woman Accused of Voter Fraud Goes on Trial," *Star-Telegram*, February 7, 2017, updated February 7, 2017, http://www.star-telegram.com/news/local/community/fort-worth/article131365129.html.
23. Petitions for Review of Orders of the Board of Immigration Appeals No. A097 846 616, in the United States Court of Appeals for the Seventh Circuit, accessed April 17, 2018, http://media.ca7.uscourts.gov/cgi-bin/rssExec.pl?Submit=Display&Path=Y2017/D02-13/C:15-2204:J:Easterbrook:aut:T:fnOp:N:1911733:S:0.

24. Connie Fitzpatrick, "Help Stop the Unjust Deportation of My Mom,"
     Indiegogo, accessed April 17, 2018, https://www.indiegogo.com/
     projects/help-stop-the-unjust-deportation-of-my-mom-history-
     women#/.

25. Ibid.

26. Dan D'Ambrosio, "VT Pauses Automatic Voter Registration after
     Problems," *Burlington Free Press*, February 3, 2017, updated February
     3, 2017, http://www.burlingtonfreepress.com/story/news/2017/02/03/
     vt-pauses-automatic-voter-registration-after-problems/97454818/.

27. Ibid.

28. Brendan Kirby, "Potentially Thousands of Illegal Voters in
     Pennsylvania," *PoliZette*, updated October 11, 2016, https://www.
     lifezette.com/polizette/potentially-thousands-illegal-voters-
     pennsylvania/.

29. Miriam Hill, Andrew Seidman, and John Duchneskie, "In 59
     Philadelphia Voting Divisions, Mitt Romney Got Zero Votes,"
     Inquirer, updated November 4, 2015, http://www.philly.com/philly/
     news/politics/20121112_In_59_Philadelphia_voting_wards__Mitt_
     Romney_got_zero_votes.html.

30. Ibid.

31. Office of Al Schimdt, City Commissioner of Philadelphia, *Voting
     Irregularities in Philadelphia County, 2012 Primary Election*, July
     2012, https://www.pagop.org/wp-content/uploads/2012/07/Voting-
     Irregularities-Report.pdf.

32. Chris Brennan, "Glitch Let Ineligible Immigrants Vote in Philly
     Elections, Officials Say," *Philadelphia Inquirer*, updated September
     20, 2017, http://www.philly.com/philly/news/politics/city/philly-voter-
     fraud-trump-immigrants-registration-commissioners-
     penndot-20170920.html.

33. Chris Brennan, "Pedro Cortes, Pa. Secretary of State, Steps Down,"
     Inquirer, updated October 11, 2017, http://www.philly.com/philly/
     news/politics/pedro-cortes-resigns-pennsylvania-secretary-of-state-
     voters-20171011.html.

34. Angela Couloumbis, "Former Pa. Election Czar Was Fired, Records
     Show," *Inquirer*, November 20, 2017, http://www.philly.com/philly/

news/politics/pedro-cortes-ousted-gov-wolf-secretary-state-20171120.html.

35. Brendan Kirby, "Potentially Thousands of Illegal Voters in Pennsylvania," *PoliZette*, updated October 11, 2016, https://www.lifezette.com/polizette/potentially-thousands-illegal-voters-pennsylvania/.

36. DCLeaks Soros docs.

37. Brendan Kirby, "Potentially Thousands of Illegal Voters in Pennsylvania," *PoliZette*, updated October 11, 2016, https://www.lifezette.com/polizette/potentially-thousands-illegal-voters-pennsylvania/.

38. Chris Brenan, "Pedro Cortes, Pa. Secretary of State, Steps Down," *Philadelphia Inquirer*, updated October 11, 2017, http://www.philly.com/philly/news/politics/pedro-cortes-resigns-pennsylvania-secretary-of-state-voters-20171011.html.

39. Ibid.

40. Presentation on Noncitizens Registered to Vote in Pennsylvania, http://www.legis.state.pa.us/WU01/LI/TR/Transcripts/2017_0109T.pdf.

41. Public Interest Legal Foundation, *Aliens & Felons: Thousands on the Voter Rolls in Philadelphia*, http://www.defendelectionintegrity.org/wp-content/uploads/2016/07/Philadelphia-Litigation-Report-Camera.pdf, p. 1.

42. Brendan Kirby, "Pennsylvania Officials Accused of Hiding Data on Noncitizen Voting," *PoliZette*, updated February 27, 2018, https://www.lifezette.com/polizette/pennsylvania-accused-of-hiding-data-on-noncitizen-voting/.

43. Public Interest Legal Foundation, *Alien Invasion in Virginia: The Discovery and Coverup of Noncitizen Registration and Voting*, September 30, 2016 https://publicinterestlegal.org/files/Report_Alien-Invasion-in-Virginia.pdf, p. 12.

44. Naomi Jagoda, "IRS Has Illegal Immigration and Taxes Problem," *Hill*, April 12, 2016, http://thehill.com/policy/finance/276086-irs-mulling-how-to-address-illegal-immigrants-using-others-identities.

45. Robert W. Wood, "IRS Admits It Encourages Illegals to Steal Social Security Numbers for Taxes," Forbes, April 13, 2016, https://www.

forbes.com/sites/robertwood/2016/04/13/irs-admits-it-encourages-illegals-to-steal-social-security-numbers-for-taxes/#22a0e9df4c04.

46. Press Release, Treasury Inspector General for Tax Administration, September 1, 2011, https://www.treasury.gov/tigta/press/press_tigta-2011-52.htm; Treasury Inspector General for Tax Administration, Recover Act, Individuals Who Are Not Authorized to Work in the United States Were Paid $4.2 Billion in Refundable Credits, July 7, 2011, https://www.treasury.gov/tigta/auditreports/2011reports/2011 41061fr.pdf.

47. Stephen Dinan, "IRS Finally Admits Illegals Can Get Back Taxes under Obama Amnesty," *Washington Times*, June 3, 2015, https://www.washingtontimes.com/news/2015/jun/3/irs-illegals-can-get-back-taxes-obama-amnesty/.

48. "Illegal Alien from Mexico Pleads Guilty in Iowa to Passport Fraud, Identity Theft, Harboring and Unlawfully Voting in a Federal Election," U.S. Immigration and Customs Enforcement, November 4, 2014, https://www.ice.gov/news/releases/illegal-alien-mexico-pleads-guilty-iowa-passport-fraud-identity-theft-harboring-and.

49. "Anchorage Man Sentenced for Falsely Claiming US Citizenship," U.S. Immigration and Customs Enforcement, March 24, 2011, https://www.ice.gov/news/releases/anchorage-man-sentenced-falsely-claiming-us-citizenship.

50. Ibid.

51. "Illegal Alien Arrested, Charged with Voter Fraud," U.S. Immigration and Customs Enforcement, March 17, 2011, https://www.ice.gov/news/releases/illegal-alien-arrested-charged-voter-fraud.

52. "ERO Baltimore Arrests Registered Sex Offender Sentenced in Illegal Identity Document, Social Security Fraud Scheme," U.S. Immigration and Customs Enforcement, March 7, 2014, https://www.ice.gov/news/releases/ero-baltimore-arrests-registered-sex-offender-sentenced-illegal-identity-document.

53. "Illegal Alien from Mexico Pleads Guilty in Iowa to Passport Fraud, Identity Theft, Harboring and Unlawfully Voting in a Federal Election," U.S. Immigration and Customs Enforcement, November 4, 2014, https://www.ice.gov/news/releases/illegal-alien-mexico-pleads-guilty-iowa-passport-fraud-identity-theft-harboring-and.

54. "Previously Deported Criminal Alien Pleads Guilty to Voter Fraud, Illegal Reentry and Falsely Claiming US Citizenship, U.S. Immigration and Customs Enforcement website, September 7, 2012, https://www. ice.gov/news/releases/previously-deported-criminal-alien-pleads-guilty-voter-fraud-illegal-reentry-and.

55. Adam B. Cos and Cristina Rodriguez, "The President and Immigration Law," Social Science Research Network, March 13, 2009, https:// papers.ssrn.com/sol3/papers.cfm?abstract_id=1356963.

56. Matt Mayer, "Obama Administration Must Enforce America's Immigration Laws," Heritage Foundation, August 26, 2010, http:// www.heritage.org/immigration/report/obama-administration-must-enforce-americas-immigration-laws.

57. Ibid.

58. Jessica M. Vaughan, "ICE Deportations Hit 10-Year Low," Center for Immigration Studies, January 11, 2017, https://cis.org/ICE-deportations-hit-10-yr-low.

59. se are mitú, "EXCLUSIVE: Gina Rodriguez Interviews President Obama – mitú," November 4, 2016, https://www.youtube.com/watch?v=oLLt-a6dI_0&feature=youtu.be.

60. Nolan D. McCaskill, "Trump Says Illegal Immigrants Pouring across the Border to Vote," *Politico*, October 7, 2016, https://www.politico.com/story/2016/10/trump-immigrants-pouring-over-border-to-vote-229274.

61. http://webcache.googleusercontent.com/search?q=cache:OwueqAq8K2gJ:www.bpunion.org/legislative-affairs/77-national%3Fstart%3D44+&cd=1&hl=en&ct=clnk&gl=us&client=opera.

62. "Obama Allots $19 Mil to Register Immigrant Voters," Judicial Watch Blog Corruption Chronicles, April 18, 2016, https://www.judicialwatch.org/blog/2016/04/obama-allots-19-mil-to-register-immigrant-voters/.

63. About NBPC, http://www.bpunion.org/about-nbpc.

64. Testimony of Art Del Cueto, National Border Patrol Council, May 9, 2016, http://docs.house.gov/meetings/HM/HM11/20160509/104818/HMTG-114-HM11-Wstate-DelCuetoA-20160509.pdf.

65. Jesse T. Richman, "Do Non-Citizens Vote in U.S. Elections?," Department of Political Science, Old Dominion University, https://ww2.odu.edu/~jrichman/NonCitizenVote.pdf.

66. http://www.sciencedirect.com/science/article/pii/S0261379414000973.

67. Jesse Richmand and David Earnest, "Could Non-Citizens Decide the November Election?," *Washington Post*, October 24, 2014, https://www.washingtonpost.com/news/monkey-cage/wp/2014/10/24/could-non-citizens-decide-the-november-election/?utm_term=.8d0a9baa4809 .

68. YouGov, https://cces.gov.harvard.edu/links/yougov.

69. Richman, "Do Non-Citizens Vote."

70. Jesse Richman and David Earnest, "Do Non-Citizens Vote in U.S. Elections? A Reply to Our Critics.," *Washington Post*, November 2, 2014, https://www.washingtonpost.com/news/monkey-cage/wp/2014/11/02/do-non-citizens-vote-in-u-s-elections-a-reply-to-our-critics/?utm_term=.a5550a8eeeac.

71. Stephen Ansolabehere, Samantha Luks, and Brian F. Schaffner, "The Perils of Cherry Picking Low Frequency Events in Large Sample Surveys," Cooperative Congressional Election Study, November 5, 2014, https://cces.gov.harvard.edu/news/perils-cherry-picking-low-frequency-events-large-sample-surveys.

72. Donor Lookup, OpenSecrets.org, https://www.opensecrets.org/donor-lookup/results?name=samantha+luks&cycle=&state=&zip=&employ y=&cand.

73. Donor Lookup, OpenSecrets.org, Brian Schaffner, https://www.opensecrets.org/donor-lookup/results?name=Brian+Schaffner.

74. Open Letter, https://assets.documentcloud.org/documents/3539975/Openletter.pdf.

75. Jesse Richman, David C. Earnest, and Gulshan Chattha, "A Valid Analysis of a Small Subsample: The Case of Non-Citizen Registration and Voting," February 7, 2017, https://fs.wp.odu.edu/jrichman/wp-content/uploads/sites/760/2015/11/AnsolabehererResponse_2-8-17.pdf.

76. Immigration, Just Facts, http://www.justfacts.com/immigration.asp#_ftn1011.

77. Rowan Scarborough, "Study Supports Trump: 5.7 Million Noncitizens May Have Cast Illegal Votes," *Washington Times*, June 19. 2017, https://www.washingtontimes.com/news/2017/jun/19/noncitizen-illegal-vote-number-higher-than-estimat/.

78. James D. Agresti, "Substantial Numbers of Non-Citizens Vote Illegally in U.S. Elections," Just Facts, December 16, 2016, http://www.justfactsdaily.com/substantial-numbers-of-non-citizens-vote-illegally-in-u-s-elections/.

79. Jesse Richman, "I Do Not Support the Washington Times Piece," Old Dominion University website, January 27, 2017, updated January 31, 2017, https://fs.wp.odu.edu/jrichman/2017/01/27/i-do-not-support-the-washington-times-piece/.

80. James D. Agresti, "Substantial Numbers of Non-Citizens Vote Illegally in U.S. Elections," Just Facts, December 16, 2016, http://www.justfactsdaily.com/substantial-numbers-of-non-citizens-vote-illegally-in-u-s-elections/.

Chapter 5 Fraud by Mail—the Problem with Absentee Ballots

1. Jack Sullivan, "The Whallen Brothers Ran Politics in 'Whiskey City,'" Those Pre-Pro Whiskey Men!, January 29, 2014, https://pre-prowhiskeymen.blogspot.com/2014/01/the-whallen-brothers-ran-politics-in_29.html.

2. Ibid.

3. "How to Steal an Election," *Kentucky Humanities*, April 2006, https://web.archive.org/web/20070330092004/http://www.kyhumanities.org/docs/6525WEB.pd.

4. Adam Liptak, "Error and Fraud at Issue as Absentee Voting Rises," *New York Times*, October 6, 2012, http://www.nytimes.com/2012/10/07/us/politics/as-more-vote-by-mail-faulty-ballots-could-impact-elections.html.

5. Ibid.

6. Ibid.

7. Ibid.

8. Ibid.

9. Sarah Fenske, "Challengers to Hubbard Family Demand Action after Detailing "Extreme Irregularities" in Absentee Ballots," *Riverfront*

Times, July 13, 2016, https://www.riverfronttimes.com/
newsblog/2016/07/13/challengers-to-hubbard-family-demand-action-
after-detailing-extreme-irregularities-in-absentee-ballots.

10. Jason Rosenbaum, "As Re-Do Election Looms in 78th District,
Hubbard Breaks Her Silence," St. Louis Public Radio, September 9,
2016, http://news.stlpublicradio.org/post/re-do-election-looms-78th-
district-hubbard-breaks-her-silence#stream/0.

11. Stephen Deere and Doug Moore, "P-D Investigation Reveals Multiple
Problems with Absentee Voting," *St. Louis Post-Dispatch*, August 31,
2016, http://www.stltoday.com/news/local/crime-and-courts/p-d-
investigation-reveals-multiple-problems-with-absentee-voting/article_
e1adc2da-3463-576d-bcdf-88acc8de5d96.html.

12. Ibid.

13. Ibid.

14. Doug Moore and Stephen Deere, "Franks Wins Big in Re-Do Election
for 78th District State Representative Seat," *St. Louis Post-Dispatch*,
September 17, 2016, http://www.stltoday.com/news/local/govt-and-
politics/franks-wins-big-in-re-do-election-for-th-district/
article_2e4cee53-10ff-5f16-873b-3912fb4c3703.html.

15. Sarah Fenske, "Penny Hubbard Ekes Out a Victory—for Now—
against Activist Bruce Franks," *Riverfront Times*, August 2, 2016,
https://www.riverfronttimes.com/newsblog/2016/08/02/penny-
hubbard-ekes-out-a-victory-for-now-against-activist-bruce-franks.

16. Ibid.

17. Robert Patrick, "Former Missouri Representative Profited in St. Louis
'Sham,'" *St. Louis Post-Dispatch*, August 22, 2012, http://www.
stltoday.com/news/local/crime-and-courts/former-missouri-
representative-profited-in-st-louis-sham/article_59f6570d-06cc-509c-
8556-98ad4fb0c9f4.html.

18. Stephen Deere and Dough Moore, "P-D Investigation Reveals Multiple
Problems with Absentee Voting," *St. Louis Post-Dispatch*, August 31,
2016, http://www.stltoday.com/news/local/crime-and-courts/p-d-
investigation-reveals-multiple-problems-with-absentee-voting/article_
e1adc2da-3463-576d-bcdf-88acc8de5d96.html.

19. William Dean Hinton, "Welcome to (Ch)eatonville," *Orlando Weekly*, November 7, 2002, https://www.orlandoweekly.com/orlando/welcome-to-cheatonville/Content?oid=2261085.

20. Tim Freed, "Former Mayor Bruce Mount to Contest Eatonville Election Results," *West Orange Times & Observer*, March 18, 2015, https://www.orangeobserver.com/article/former-mayor-bruce-mount-contest-eatonville-election-results.

21. Ryan Gillespie, "Former Eatonville Mayor Found Guilty of Voting Fraud, Election Violations," *Orlando Sentinel*, May 19, 2017, http://www.orlandosentinel.com/news/breaking-news/os-anthony-grant-trial-verdict-20170519-story.html.

22. Steven Lemongello, "Former Mayor Alleges Fraud, Bribery by Grant in Eatonville Election," *Orlando Sentinel*, March 26, 2015, http://www.orlandosentinel.com/news/breaking-news/os-eatonville-election-lawsuit-20150326-story.html.

23. Emilee Speck, "Prosecution Compares Pop-Tarts to Ballots in Ex Eatonville Mayor's Fraud Trial," WKMG-TV, May 19, 2017, updated May 19, 2017, https://www.clickorlando.com/news/jury-deliberating-in-former-eatonville-mayor-voter-fraud-case.

24. Lawrence Mower, Lulu Ramadan, Alexandra Seltzer, and Justin Price, "EXCLUSIVE: Winning Candidates Helped Voters Fill Out Their Ballots," *Palm Beach Post*, March 10, 2017, http://www.mypalmbeachpost.com/news/special-reports/exclusive-winning-candidates-helped-voters-fill-out-their-ballots/V0ieae6VcZNNWF6I9ylRdM/.

25. Ibid.

26. Ibid.

27. Ibid.

28. Lawrence Mower, "EXCLUSIVE: Voter Fraud in Palm Beach County: State Attorney Finds Crimes, but no Suspect," *Palm Beach Post*, July 23, 2017, http://www.mypalmbeachpost.com/news/exclusive-voter-fraud-palm-beach-county-state-attorney-finds-crimes-but-suspect/buShkHum7thKuTKE8F69QO/.

29. Lawrence Mower, "Democratic Politician Rips Post's Coverage of Absentee Ballot Fraud," *Palm Beach Post*, July 26, 2017, http://www.

palmbeachpost.com/news/democratic-politician-rips-post-coverage-absentee-ballot-fraud/OCfboh8NrdZjgv2FS3MzVO/.

30. Lawrence Mower, Lulu Ramadan, Alexandra Seltzer, and Justin Price, "EXCLUSIVE: Winning Candidates Helped Voters Fill Out Their Ballots," *Palm Beach Post*, March 10, 2017, http://www.mypalmbeachpost.com/news/special-reports/exclusive-winning-candidates-helped-voters-fill-out-their-ballots/V0ieae6VcZNNWF6I9ylRdM/.

31. Voter Fraud Close Out document, June 22, 217, https://www.documentcloud.org/documents/3898475-Voter-Fraud-Close-Out-16PI000030A99-Redacted.html.

32. Melissa Sanchez and Enrique Flor, "Hialeah Ballot Broker's Notes List Candidates' Names, Payments," *Miami Herald*, May 12, 2013, updated September 8, 2014, http://www.miamiherald.com/latest-news/article1951480.html.

33. "In Ro Grande Valley, Some Campaign Workers Are Paid to Harvest Votes, National Public Radio, July 7, 2015, https://www.npr.org/2015/07/07/413463879/in-rio-grande-valley-some-campaign-workers-are-paid-to-harvest-votes?utm_medium=RSS&utm_campaign=storiesfromnpr.

34. https://www.nexis.com/results/enhdocview.do?docLinkInd=true&ersKey=23_T27146690902&format=GNBFI&startDocNo=1&resultsUrlKey=0_T27146766067&backKey=20_T27146766068&csi=172244&docNo=2

35. Turnout and Voter Registration Figures (1970–current), Texas Secretary of State website, accessed April 18, 2018, https://www.sos.state.tx.us/elections/historical/70-92.shtml. Numbers collected from the records of four counties in the McAllen and Brownsville divisions, and averaged. Individual percentages are: Hidalgo (51 percent), Willacy (41 percent), Cameron (46 percent), and Starr (36 percent).

36. Aliseda testified that Texas Rangers were sent to Bee County to investigate fraud allegations and declared no fraud. Aliseda later found that the Rangers had been golfing with one of the suspects of the investigation at the municipal golf course. The Texas Rangers were sent back after Aliseda shared this information with their supervisor

and later uncovered four cases of fraud. *Texas v. Eric Holder*, http://
www.campaignlegalcenter.org/sites/default/files/070912texasam.pdf
37. Not sure if this is the colloquial name/correct abbreviation for the case,
but either way this is the plaintiff/defendant.
38. Ibid.
39. Steve Miller, "Politiquero Tradition Shapes Elections in South Texas,"
Texas Watchdog, April 7, 2010, http://moritzlaw.osu.edu/electionlaw/
litigation/documents/TexasWatchdogArticle.pdf.
40. https://www.nexis.com/results/enhdocview.
do?docLinkInd=true&ersKey=23_T27146690902&format=GNBFI
&startDocNo=1&resultsUrlKey=0_T27146766067&backKey=20_
T27146766068&csi=172244&docNo=2.
41. "In Rio Grande Valley, Some Campaign Workers Are Paid to Harvest
Votes," National Public Radio, July 7, 2015, https://www.npr.
org/2015/07/07/413463879/in-rio-grande-valley-some-campaign-
workers-are-paid-to-harvest-votes?utm_medium=RSS&utm_
campaign=storiesfromnpr.
42. Erin Vogel-Fox, Michael Olinger, "Reports to the Federal Government
about Military Voting Often Are Flawed," Center for Public Integrity,
August 26, 2016, https://www.publicintegrity.org/2016/08/26/20085/
reports-federal-government-about-military-voting-often-are-flawed.

Chapter 6 Who's Running This Thing Anyways?—The Counters
1. "Montana Gov. Brian Schweitzer Speech to Trial Lawyers Convention,
7/14/2008," July 14, 2008, https://archive.org/details/MontanaGov.
BrianSchweitzerSpeechToTrialLawyersConvention7142008.
2. Jennifer McKee, "Schweitzer 'Joke' May Have Grain of Truth,"
Billings Gazette, September 10, 2008, http://billingsgazette.com/news/
state-and-regional/montana/schweitzer-joke-may-have-grain-of-truth/
article_850f5831-8b25-5632-af0f-9dc00457bb1f.html.
3. Kirk Johnson, "Montana Officials Chastise Governor Over Boasts in
Speech to Lawyers' Group," *New York Times*, September 11, 2008,
http://www.nytimes.com/2008/09/12/us/12montana.html.
4. Drew Cline, "Drew Cline: Bill Gardner Knows That Voter Fraud
Happens in New Hampshire," *Union Leader*, September 24, 2014,

http://www.unionleader.com/apps/pbcs.dll/article?AID=/20140925/
LOCALVOICES03/140929402&template=printart.

5. Office of the Minnesota Secretary of State Steve Simon website, http://
www.sos.state.mn.us/elections-voting/register-to-vote/register-on-
election-day/.

6. "Preliminary Findings of Joint Task Force Investigating Possible
Election Fraud," May 10, 2005, http://p2004.org/states/
wifraud051005.html.

7. "Election Administration at State and Local Levels," National
Conference of State Legislatures, June 15, 2016, http://www.ncsl.org/
research/elections-and-campaigns/election-administration-at-state-
and-local-levels.aspx.

8. Letter from Chris Millis to Elaine Marshall, http://nchouse16.com/
docs/millis-marshall-march27.pdf; *See also* Lauren Horsch, "NC's
Secretary of State Takes Heat over Immigrant Notaries," *News &
Observer*, March 28, 2017, updated March 28, 2017, http://www.
newsobserver.com/news/politics-government/politics-columns-blogs/
under-the-dome/article141358578.html.

9. Associated Press, "Florida Voter Rolls Suspected of Having Roughly
53K Dead, 2,600 Ineligible," Fox News, May 17, 2012, http://www.
foxnews.com/politics/2012/05/17/florida-voter-rolls-suspected-
having-roughly-53k-dead-2600-ineligible.html.

10. Public Interest Legal Foundation, https://publicinterestlegal.org/
reports/.

11. Max Greenwood, "Kentucky Secretary of State: 'Not Enough Bourbon
in Kentucky' to Make Me Release Voter Data," *Hill*, June 30, 2017,
http://thehill.com/homenews/state-watch/340331-kentucky-secretary-
of-state-not-enough-bourbon-in-kentucky-to-make-me.

12. Deroy Murdock, "Necessary Hygiene," *National Review*, June 18,
2012, https://www.nationalreview.com/2012/06/necessary-hygiene-
deroy-murdock/.

13. Laura Vozzella, "Va. Gov. McAuliffe Says He Has Broken U.S. Record
for Restoring Voting Rights," *Washington Post*, April 27, 2017, https://
www.washingtonpost.com/local/virginia-politics/
va-gov-mcauliffe-says-he-has-broken-us-record-for-restoring-voting-

rights/2017/04/27/55b5591a-2b8b-11e7-be51-b3fc6ff7faee_story.
html?noredirect=on&utm_term=.824388afac6d.

14. Deroy Murdock, "Ghost Voters," *National Review*, August 11, 2017,
     https://www.nationalreview.com/2017/08/election-fraud-registered-
     voters-outnumber-eligible-voters-462-counties/.

15. Rose Gill Hearn, *New York City Department of Investigation Report
     on the New York City Board of Elections' Employment Practices,
     Operations, and Election Administration*, December 2013, http://
     www1.nyc.gov/assets/doi/reports/pdf/2013/2013-12-30-BOE_Unit_
     Report.pdf.

16. Ibid.

17. Orli Santo, "Brooklyn Hasidim Face Accusations of Voter Fraud,"
     Times of Israel, September 13, 2013, https://www.timesofisrael.com/
     brooklyn-hasidim-face-accusations-of-longtime-voter-fraud/.

18. Ibid.

19. http://gothamist.com/2013/09/11/voter_fraud_attempts.php.

20. "About the Supervisor," https://www.browardsoe.org/Your-Election-
     Office/About-the-Supervisor.

21. John Mercurio, "Jeb Bush Removes Broward County Elections Chief,"
     CNN, November 20, 2003, http://www.cnn.com/2003/
     ALLPOLITICS/11/20/florida.election/.

22. Problems with absentee ballots in Florida NPR All Things Considered
     (NPR) October 28, 2004, Thursday.

23. David Sutta, "Broward Elections Dept. under Fire," CBS Miami,
     November 16, 2012, http://miami.cbslocal.com/2012/11/16/broward-
     elections-dept-under-fire/.

24. Brittany Wallman, "Mayor: Illegal Voters Still Voting in Broward,"
     Sun-Sentinel, October 9, 2012, http://www.sun-sentinel.com/local/
     broward/broward-politics-blog/sfl-broward-illegal-voters-still-voting-
     in-broward-20121009-story.html.

25. Tom Lauder, "Broward County Creates Phantom District to Allow
     Illegal Voting," Media Trackers, April 30, 2014, http://mediatrackers.
     org/2014/04/30/broward-county-creates-phantom-district-to-allow-
     illegal-voting/.

26. Susannah Bryan, "Convicted Felon May Not Be Eligible for Dania Commission Seat," *Sun-Sentinel*, September 24, 2014, http://www. sun-sentinel.com/news/fl-dania-candidate-felon-20140924-story.html.

27. Sun Sentinel Editorial Board, "Embarrassments Keep Coming at Election Time," *Sun-Sentinel*, September 30, 2014, http://www.sun-sentinel.com/opinion/editorials/fl-editorial-dania-gs-20140930-story. html.

28. Kyoto Walker, "Ascension of an Election Supervisor," *South Florida Times*, February 12, 2015–February 18, 2015.

29. Sun Sentinel Editorial Board, "Clear Ethics Cloud over Elections Office," *Sun-Sentinel*, June 8, 2015, http://www.sun-sentinel.com/ opinion/editorials/fl-editorial-supervisor-elections-brenda-snipes-20150608-story.html.

30. Amy Sherman, "Broward Prosecutors Reviewing Elections Office Posting Results Early," *Miami Herald*, August 31, 2016, updated August 31, 2016, http://www.miamiherald.com/news/local/ community/broward/article99026372.html.

31. Antonia Noori Farzan, "Here's Everything That's Gone Wrong for Broward's Supervisor of Elections This Year," *New Times Broward-Palm Beach*, November 8, 2016, http://www.browardpalmbeach.com/ news/here-s-everything-that-s-gone-wrong-for-broward-s-supervisor-of-elections-this-year-8215428.

32. Anthony Man, "Congressional Candidate Accuses Elections Chief of Wrongly Destroying 2016 Ballots," *Sun-Sentinel*, December 15, 2017, http://www.sun-sentinel.com/news/politics/fl-reg-tim-canova-brenda-snipes-clash-20171215-story.html.

33. "Affidavit of Chelsey Marie Smith," http://6889-presscdn-0-68.pagely. netdna-cdn.com/wp-content/uploads/2016/11/Chelsey-Smith-SOE-Affidavit.pdf.

34. Todd Beamon, "Florida Elections Worker: I Was Fired for Witnessing Possible Absentee Ballot Fraud," Newsmax, November 4, 2016, https://www.newsmax.com/t/newsmax/article/757191?section=New sfront&keywords=florida-elections-worker-alleges&year=2016&mo nth=11&date=04&id=757191&aliaspath=%2FManage%2FArticles %2FTemplate-Main.

35. Larry Barszewski, "Broward Elections Supervisor Makes Changes after Being Sued," *Sun-Sentinel*, July 31, 2017, http://www.sun-sentinel.com/local/broward/fl-sb-broward-election-supervisor-testifies-20170728-story.html.

Chapter 7 Double-Barreled Voter Fraud

1. Greg Reeves, "People Voting Twice in Kansas, Missouri," *Billings Gazette*, September 5, 2004, http://billingsgazette.com/news/national/people-voting-twice-in-kansas-missouri/article_b6c981e6-d886-5427-9896-d59fea05aa31.html.
2. Ibid.
3. Ibid.
4. Russ Buettner, "Exposed: Scandal of Double Voters: 46,000 Registered to Vote in City & Fla.," *New York Daily News*, August 22, 2004, http://www.nydailynews.com/archives/news/exposed-scandal-double-voters-46-000-registered-vote-city-fla-article-1.569992.
5. Roger Roy and Beth Kassab, "Double Votes Taint Florida, Records Show," *Orlando Sentinel*, October 22, 2004, http://articles.orlandosentinel.com/2004-10-22/news/0410220246_1_databases-registered-to-vote-double-voters.
6. Emily Rittman and Nick Sloan, "Wyandotte County Man Charged with Double-Voting; Kobach Talks Illegal Voting," KCTV5 News, November 7, 2017, updated December 7, 2017, http://www.kctv5.com/story/36789859/wyandotte-county-man-charged-with-double-voting-kobach-talks-illegal-voting.
7. Ibid.
8. Natalie St. John, "Former GOP Candidate Charged with Felony Vote Fraud," *Chinook Observer*, October 9, 2017, http://www.chinookobserver.com/co/local-news/20171009/former-gop-candidate-charged-with-felony-vote-fraud.
9. News Release, "Secretary of State Forwards Cases of Potential Voter Fraud to County Prosecutors," Secretary of State Kim Wyman website, September 15, 2017, https://www.sos.wa.gov/office/news-releases.aspx#/news/1252.

10. Sharad Goel, Marc Meredith, Michael Morse, David Rothschild, and Houshmand Shirani-Mehr, *One Person, One Vote: Estimating the Prevalence of Double Voting in U.S. Presidential Elections*, October 24, 2017, https://5harad.com/papers/1p1v.pdf.

11. Michael Gerstein, "Six Months Later, AG Probe into Double Voting Drags On," *Detroit News*, August 11, 2017, http://www.detroitnews.com/story/news/politics/2017/08/11/double-voting/104496150/.

12. Jesse Paul, "10 People in Colorado May Have Cast Two Ballots in 2016 Election, While 38 Might Have Also Voted in Another State, Study Says," *Denver Post*, September 15, 2017, updated September 15, 2017, https://www.denverpost.com/2017/09/15/colorado-2016-improper-voting-study/.

13. "Nashville Election Worker Fired over Double Voting," *Tennessean*, May 12, 2014, updated May 12, 2014, https://www.tennessean.com/story/news/politics/2014/05/12/election-officials-weigh-double-voting/9013815/.

14. Eric Shawn, "Double-Voting—Even Trip-Voting—Found in US Elections," Fox News, September 12, 2016 http://www.foxnews.com/politics/2016/09/12/double-voting-even-triple-voting-found-in-us-elections.html.

15. Ibid.

16. Michael Dresser, "Official in Md., Va., Investigate Report That 164 Voted in Both States," *Baltimore Sun*, August 28, 2014, http://www.baltimoresun.com/news/maryland/politics/bs-md-election-referrals-20140828-story.html.

17. "Double Voting? Not Necessarily [Editorial]," *Baltimore Sun*, September 2, 2014, http://www.baltimoresun.com/news/opinion/editorial/bs-ed-voter-fraud-20140902-story.html.

18. Felony Crimes, Richard E. Hornsby, P.A., website, accessed April 19, 2018, https://www.richardhornsby.com/crimes/felony.html.

19. Electronic Registration Information Center website, accessed April 19, 2018, http://www.ericstates.org/.

20. J. Christian Adams, "Leaked Documents Reveal Expansive Soros Funding to Manipulate Federal Elections," PJ Media, November 7, 2016, https://pjmedia.com/jchristianadams/2016/11/07/

leaked-documents-reveal-expansive-soros-funding-to-manipulate-federal-elections/.

21.   "Voter List Accuracy, National Conference of State Legislatures website, June 6, 2016, http://www.ncsl.org/research/elections-and-campaigns/voter-list-accuracy.aspx.

22.   For a detailed description of the methodology behind the study, go to the GAI's investigations website: https://www.g-a-i.org/investigations/.

23.   John Hayward, "Kris Kobach: GAI Report Backs Up My Findings on Under-Prosecuted Crime of Double Voting," *Breitbart*, July 27, 2017, http://www.breitbart.com/radio/2017/07/27/kris-kobach-gai-report-backs-findings-prosecuted-crime-double-voting/.

24.   Associated Press, "The Oldest Person in America Has Died," *New York Post*, February 9, 2017, https://nypost.com/2017/02/09/the-oldest-person-in-america-has-died/.

25.   2000 Official Presidential General Election Results, November 7, 2000, updated December 2001, https://transition.fec.gov/pubrec/2000presgeresults.htm.

26.   "Provisional Voting," Moritz College of Law, Ohio State University, website, accessed April 19, 2018, http://moritzlaw.osu.edu/electionlaw/ebook/part5/hava.html.

27.   "The Problem of Duplicate Voting," GAI Report Rhode Island emails (Appendix C), http://g-a-i.org/wp-content/uploads/2017/07/Voter-Fraud-Final-with-Appendix-1.pdf.

28.   2013 Rhode Island General Laws, Justia, accessed April 19, 2018, https://law.justia.com/codes/rhode-island/2013/title-17/chapter-17-9.1/section-17-9.1-29/.

Chapter 8 Who Counts the Votes?

1.   Victoria Collier, "How to Rig an Election," *Harper's Magazine*, November 2012, https://harpers.org/archive/2012/11/how-to-rig-an-election/3/.

2.   Nick Gass, "Study: Electronic Voting Machines in 43 States Are out of Date," *Politico*, September 9, 2015, https://www.politico.com/story/2015/09/study-electronic-voting-machines-out-of-date-43-states-213632.

3.   Interview with author.

4. Nick Gass, "Study: Electronic Voting Machines in 43 States Are out of Date," *Politico*, September 9, 2015, https://www.politico.com/story/2015/09/study-electronic-voting-machines-out-of-date-43-states-213632.

5. Doug McDonough, "County Might Replace Aging Voting Machines," *Plainview Herald*, July 18, 2017, http://www.myplainview.com/news/article/County-might-replace-aging-voting-machines-11297573.php.

6. Chad Livengood and Joel Kurth, "Half of Detroit Votes May Be Ineligible for Recount," *Detroit News*, December 5, 2016, http://www.detroitnews.com/story/news/politics/2016/12/05/recount-unrecountable/95007392/.

7. Brandie Kessler, Teresa Boeckel, and Dylan Segelbaum, "'Redo' of Some York County Races—Including Judge—Possible after Voting Problems," *York Daily Record*, November 7, 2017, updated November 7, 2017, https://www.ydr.com/story/news/2017/11/07/problem-york-county-voting-machines-could-allow-extra-votes-some-candidates/841010001/.

8. David DeMille, "Voting Machine Issues Complicate Balloting in Washington County," *Spectrum*, November 8, 2016, updated November 8, 2016, http://www.thespectrum.com/story/news/2016/11/08/election-machine-problems-early-washington-county/93470912/.

9. Pam Fessler, "Some Machines Are Flipping Votes, but That Doesn't Mean They're Rigged," National Public Radio, October 26, 2016, https://www.npr.org/2016/10/26/499450796/some-machines-are-flipping-votes-but-that-doesnt-mean-theyre-rigged.

10. Ibid.

11. Kim Zetter, "The Myth of the Hacker-Proof Voting Machine," *New York Times*, February 21, 2018, https://www.nytimes.com/2018/02/21/magazine/the-myth-of-the-hacker-proof-voting-machine.html.

12. Ibid.

13. Ibid.

14. A. J. Vicens, "State Voter Registration Systems Are Easier to Hack Than Anyone Wants to Admit," Mother Jones, August 2, 2017, https://

www.motherjones.com/politics/2017/08/state-voter-registration-systems-are-easier-to-hack-than-anyone-wants-to-admit/.

15. Cynthia McFadden, William M. Arkin, Kevin Monahan, and Ken Dilanian, "U.S. Intel: Russia Compromised Seven States Prior to 2016 Election," NBC News, February 27, 2018, updated February 28, 2018, https://www.nbcnews.com/politics/elections/u-s-intel-russia-compromised-seven-states-prior-2016-election-n850296.

16. S.2261—Secure Elections Act, Congress.gov, accessed June 1, 2018, https://www.congress.gov/bill/115th-congress/senate-bill/2261.

17. Kim Westbook Strach, "How NC Is Meeting the Threat to Election Security," *Charlotte Observer*, February 27, 2018, updated February 27, 2018, http://www.charlotteobserver.com/opinion/op-ed/article202454724.html.

18. Colin Woodard, "U.S. Too Passive, Vulnerable to Elections Cyberthreat, Sen. King Says," *Portland Press Herald*, February 26, https://www.pressherald.com/2018/02/26/u-s-too-passive-on-cyber-threat-to-elections-remains-vulnerable-sen-king-says/.

19. Arizona Legislature website, accessed April 19, 2018, https://www.azleg.gov/ars/16/00661.htm.

20. The 2017 Florida Statutes, Online Sunshine, accessed April 19, 2018, http://www.leg.state.fl.us/statutes/index.cfm?App_mode=Display_Statute&URL=0100-0199/0102/Sections/0102.141.html.

21. Iowa Code, Iowa Legislature website, accessed April 19, 2018, https://www.legis.iowa.gov/publications/search/document?fq=id:870524&pdid=867687&q=recount#50.48.

22. "Frequently Asked Questions after an Election," Louisiana Secretary of State Tom Schedler website, accessed April 20, 2018, https://www.sos.la.gov/ElectionsAndVoting/BecomeACandidate/FrequentlyAskedQuestions/Pages/FAQsAfterAnElection.aspx?OwnershipName=CandidateInfoAfterElection&faqid=0.

23. Joel Kurth, "Botched Elections. Missing Ballots. Is This Any Way to Run a Democracy?," Detroit Journalism Cooperative, August 1, 2017, http://www.bridgemi.com/detroit-journalism-cooperative/botched-elections-missing-ballots-any-way-run-democracy.

Chapter 9 Who Cares Who Votes?

1.   Post Editorial Board, "The Election Official Who Spoke His Mind on Vote Fraud," *New York Post*, October 14, 2016, https://nypost.com/2016/10/14/the-election-official-who-spoke-his-mind-on-vote-fraud/.

2.   Carl Campanile, "Elections Official Caught on Video Blasting de Blasio's ID Program," *New York Post*, October 11, 2016, https://nypost.com/2016/10/11/elections-official-caught-on-video-blasting-de-blasios-id-program/.

3.   Rich Calder and Carl Campanile, "De Blasio Demands Resignation of Elections Official Who Blasted ID Program," *New York Post*, October 14, 2016, https://nypost.com/2016/10/14/de-blasio-demands-resignation-of-elections-official-who-blasted-id-program/.

4.   Voter Registration in North Dakota, DMV.org, accessed June 1, 2018, https://www.dmv.org/nd-north-dakota/voter-registration.php.

5.   Christopher Ingraham, "Kris Kobach Says He Can't Comply with Kris Kobach's Voter Data Request," *Washington Post*, June 30, 2017, https://www.washingtonpost.com/news/wonk/wp/2017/06/30/kris-kobach-says-hes-cant-comply-with-kris-kobachs-voter-data-request/?utm_term=.65deedb6481f.

6.   United States District Court for the District of Columbia, accessed April 20, 2018, https://www.documentcloud.org/documents/4177962-Final-Dunlap-Complaint.html.

7.   "LISTEN: Election Law Center Founder J. CHRISTIAN ADAMS on Trump Dissolving the Voter Fraud Commission: Secretary of State Matthew Dunlap Sabotaged the Commission," WMAL Radio, January 8, 2018, http://www.wmal.com/2018/01/08/listen-election-law-center-founder-j-christian-adams-on-trump-dissolving-the-voter-fraud-commission-secretary-of-state-matthew-dunlap-sabotaged-t-he-commission/.

8.   Ibid.

9.   Ibid.

10. Memorandum Opinion, United States District Court for the District of Columbia, December 22, 2017, https://www.politico.com/f/?id=00000160-80d7-da3c-a371-80ff4b980001.

11. Rachel Weiner, "Federal Court Rejects Challenge to Trump Voting Commission," *Washington Post*, December 26, 2017, https://www. washingtonpost.com/local/public-safety/federal-court-rejects-challenge-to-trump-voter-commission/2017/12/26/f1f64f42-ea61-11e7-9f92-10a2203f6c8d_story.html?utm_term=.b37971de43e9.

12. "Legal Actions Taken against Trump's 'Voter Fraud' Commission," Brennan Center for Justice, last updated December 26, 2017, https:// www.brennancenter.org/legal-actions-taken-against-trump%E2%80%99s-%E2%80%9Cfraud%E2%80%9D-commission.

13. Ibid.

14. Michael Tackett and Michael Wines, "Trump Disbands Commission on Voter Fraud," *New York Times*, January 3, 2018, https://www. nytimes.com/2018/01/03/us/politics/trump-voter-fraud-commission. html.

15. Government Accountability Institute, *America the Vulnerable: The Problem of Duplicate Voting*, accessed April 20, 2018, http://g-a-i. org/wp-content/uploads/2017/07/Voter-Fraud-Final-with-Appendix-1. pdf.

16. Katherine Gregg, "Ken Block Files Complaint Alleging R.I. Violates Federal Voting Law," *Providence Journal*, September 28, 2017, updated September 28, 2017, http://www.providencejournal.com/ news/20170928/ken-block-files-complaint-alleging-ri-violates-federal-voting-law.

17. "Help America Vote Act (HAVA) of 2002," Ballotpedia, accessed April 20, 2018, https://ballotpedia.org/Help_America_Vote_Act_ (HAVA)_of_2002.

18. QuickFacts: Central Falls City, Rhode Island, United States Census Bureau, accessed April 20, 2018, https://www.census.gov/quickfacts/ fact/table/centralfallscityrhodeisland/PST045216.

19. Rhode Island Board of Elections, *Rules and Regulations for Voter Registration*, last amended September 14, 2016, http://sos.ri.gov/ documents/archives/regdocs/released/pdf/BOE/8381.pdf.

20. Search Results: Ralph A. Mollis, OpenSecrets.org, accessed April 20, 2018, https://www.opensecrets.org/search?cof=FORID%3A11&cx=

0106779074629555562473%3Anlldkv0jvam&q=ralph+a+mollis&ty
pe=donors.

21.   Katherine Gregg, "Board of Elections Fires Embattled Executive
       Director Robert Kando," *Providence Journal*, August 31, 2016,
       updated August 31, 2016, http://www.providencejournal.com/
       news/20160831/board-of-elections-fires-embattled-executive-
       director-robert-kando.

22.   Ibid.

23.   *United States of America v. State of New Jersey and Stuart Rabner*,
       in the United States District Court for the District of New Jersey,
       accessed April 20, 2018, https://www.justice.gov/sites/default/files/crt/
       legacy/2010/12/15/nj_hava_comp.pdf.

24.   Ibid.

25.   Katherine Gregg, "R.I. Elections Board Moves to Close Voter
       Registration Loophole," *Providence Journal*, November 13, 2017,
       November 13, 2017, http://www.providencejournal.com/
       news/20171113/ri-elections-board-moves-to-close-voter-registration-
       loophole.

Chapter 10 Summing Up: Voting and Citizenship

1.   Lydia Wheeler, "Dem AGS Press Trump Officials Not to Include
       Citizenship Question in Census," *Hill*, February 12, 2018, http://
       thehill.com/regulation/administration/373450-dem-ags-press-trump-
       officials-not-to-include-citizenship-question.

2.   Press Release, "Attorney General Becerra to Trump Administration:
       Citizenship Question on 2020 Census would Be Unconstitutional,"
       State of California Department of Justice website, February 12, 2018,
       https://oag.ca.gov/news/press-releases/attorney-general-becerra-
       trump-administration-citizenship-question-2020-census.

3.   Candice Miller, "More Illegal Immigrants, More Seats in Congress?,"
       Letters to the Editor, *Washington Post*, September 11, 2007, http://
       www.washingtonpost.com/wp-dyn/content/article/2007/09/10/
       AR2007091002107.html.

4.   Ryan Baugh, "U.S. Lawful Permanent Residents: 2016, *Annual Flow
       Report*, December 2017, https://www.dhs.gov/sites/default/files/
       publications/Lawful_Permanent_Residents_2016.pdf.

5. Jeffrey S. Passel and D'Vera Cohn, "20 Metro Areas Are Home to Six-in-Ten Unauthorized Immigrants in U.S.," Pew Research Center, February 9, 2017, http://www.pewresearch.org/fact-tank/2017/02/09/us-metro-areas-unauthorized-immigrants/.

6. Leonard Steinhorn, "Without Voting, Noncitizens Could Swing the Election for Obama," *Washington Post*, October 5, 2012, https://www.washingtonpost.com/opinions/without-voting-noncitizens-could-swing-the-election-for-obama/2012/10/05/b9d99be8-0be9-11e2-bd1a-b868e65d57eb_story.html?noredirect=on&utm_term=.a902f01bb9f3.

7. Paul Goldman and Mark J. Rozell, "Illegal Immigrants Could Elect Hillary," *Politico*, October 3, 2015, https://www.politico.com/magazine/story/2015/10/illegal-immigrants-could-elect-hillary-clinton-213216.

8. Jack Heretik, "DNC Chairman Equates Census Citizenship Question to Voter Suppression," *Washington Free Beacon*, March 27, 2018, http://freebeacon.com/politics/dnc-chairman-equates-census-citizenship-question-voter-suppression/.

9. Zoltan L. Hajinal, Nazita Lajevardi, and Lindsay Nielson, "Do Voter Identification Laws Suppress Minority Voting? Yes. We Did the Research.," *Washington Post*, February 15, 2017, https://www.washingtonpost.com/news/monkey-cage/wp/2017/02/15/do-voter-identification-laws-suppress-minority-voting-yes-we-did-the-research/?utm_term=.3d2ba8ca4c8c.

10. German Lopez, "A Major Study Finding That Voter ID Laws Hurt Minorities Isn't Standing Up Well under Scrutiny," *Vox*, March 15, 2017, https://www.vox.com/identities/2017/3/15/14909764/study-voter-id-racism.

Index